MR ASQUITH, MR LAW AND THE GODDESS OF JUSTICE

John Little

Acknowledgements

I am grateful to Dr Lewis Johnman of the University of Westminster for his input, his suggestions and all his help with this book. His drawing of my attention to the Jacks case was especially useful in changing my thinking about the possible reasons for the formation of the May 1915 Coalition. His input was invaluable.

To my wife Ruth Little I owe a debt for her administrator's eye correcting my manuscript, and whipping it into a more professional presentation. For further proofing I wish to thank David Banks from Halifax, Nova Scotia for spotting more typos. I would like to acknowledge and thank the British Library or the use I have made of their collections, and for the help of their patient and very professional staff

The British Newspaper Archive is another institution I am grateful to for the use of their collections. At a period when the national newspapers were heavily censored, the regional papers were sometimes not under such a tight rein and this proved useful. Having it all online is a researcher's dream. I have used no images from their collections, but without their permission to use quotations from their material I could not have written this book.

The Parliamentary Archives I wish to thank particularly; once through the careful security of the Houses of Parliament and up an escorted lift I found a mine of useful information, especially in the Bonar Law and Lloyd George collections.

The National Archives I also thank and acknowledge for the use of material stored there, and similarly the Wiltshire Archives for use of their Walter Long collection which complements the British Library collection.

The Bodleian Library I also thank for use of the Asquith Papers.

Finally I wish to thank Jan Lettens for allowing me to use his description of the sunken Themis at the end of my work.

Preface

It is in the nature of human beings to find that events external to themselves affect their emotions, and very often their actions. There are situations in which people find themselves, either through actions of their own, or of people close to them, that prey on their minds, keep them awake at night and influence what they do, or do not do, next.

The last Liberal government of the United Kingdom ended in May 1915 in very mysterious circumstances which have been the subject of much argument ever since.

William Maxwell Aitken, later Lord Beaverbrook, a Canadian friend of Andrew Bonar Law, was in and around Westminster in the period in which the administration of Herbert Henry Asquith ended, though he was in France when it actually happened. In 1916 Aitken bought *The Daily Express* and subsequently became a press baron of great power and influence. For a long time, the account he wrote of the events surrounding the end of the Liberal government in 1915 was more or less the accepted version. In this story the leader of the Conservatives, Bonar Law, saw that the way things were going with the conduct of the war could not go on. He went to Asquith and held a metaphorical pistol to his head, threatening him with a divisive and embarrassing debate in the Commons if he did not make concessions, and Asquith caved in.

There has been a close examination of what did actually happen in mid May 1915 by many very able historians, but a definitive account is still lacking for the simple reason that Asquith had a safe majority in the House of Commons, and any conceivable challenge to him would have been doomed to failure from the start. No threat from Bonar Law, no pressure from Conservative groups or individuals, no thundering from newspapers could have budged the Prime Minister if he did not wish to be budged. Yet budge he did, and the question must arise of why he did.

Several authors have put forward the idea that Asquith had actually been moving towards a coalition, though he did not like it, because it was necessary for there to be one. This is probably true, but it only provides a part answer to the question of why he did it on 17 May, and especially as to why he did it as quickly as he did. The path towards the formation of the May Coalition is a well-trodden one, and the events have been examined minutely and well. Responsibility for bringing pressure to bear on the government has been ascribed to various people; Bonar Law, Edward Carson, Professor Hewins, Robert Cecil and Walter Long have been suggested, though the last has not been the most popular candidate. Yet the mystery of Asquith's appearing to give in without a fight and form a coalition eludes a definitive solution.

Roy Jenkins in his 1960s biography of Asquith came up with the idea that Asquith was not operating at quite his usual level on 17 May 1915 because he was emotionally upset at the ending of his friendship with a young woman, Venetia Stanley, about whom he had become obsessive. He wrote hundreds of letters to her, often at inappropriate times, and told her far too much that he should not. Asquith being human, it is a reasonable assumption that her announcement on 12 May that she was going to be married hit him hard. The nature of this relationship has been discussed many times in articles and books; was it sexual? was it 'courtly love'? was she just a 'muse'? was she a friend with whom the Prime Minister 'tossed his thoughts'? There is no hard evidence that will answer any of this satisfactorily at the moment. Certainly it has been put forward that Asquith had that feature of so many prominent politicians, that he was able to 'compartmentalize' his thoughts very well, and he kept his activities so well separated that he was able to engage in them completely untroubled by what was going on in the other 'boxes'. It may be that Venetia's engagement disturbed him; his letters indicate that it did. On the other hand it may be that it did not disturb him; that the language in the letters was no more than him letting off steam in the way he needed to.

The theory that he was emotionally weakened and gave in to Bonar Law's threats on 17 May is a factor to bear in mind. Without it, no consideration of the events leading to the formation of the 1915 coalition is complete.

There is another factor to bear in mind that has received less attention. If it is a valid exercise to bear in mind the mental state of the Prime Minister, then it is also a valid exercise to bear in mind the mental state of the leader of the Conservative Party on 17 May 1915. There are very good reasons why Andrew Bonar Law was also not a very happy man on the day the Liberal Government ended. It may well be that Asquith's mental distress must be borne in mind as a factor in ending his administration, but Bonar Law had far more reason to be both distressed and under stress. He was under extraordinary pressure in his political life, but also in his

3

personal life, and it cannot have left him unaffected. Any examination of this period that does not examine this is also incomplete.

Chapter 1

Prologue

On Friday 24 July 1914 a ship set sail for Europe. The Themis, a sturdy workhorse of the sea en route from Nova Scotia to Rotterdam with a cargo of 7500 tons of iron ore left Wabana Harbour, Newfoundland. This town of 14,000 people had mushroomed since the 1890s when underground iron ore mines had fuelled the rise of a prosperous mining industry. The Themis was one of several ships dedicated on full time charter to carry iron ore across the Atlantic, a lucrative trade for her Norwegian owners, her Dutch crew and the agents who facilitated her use; the other ships were the Tellus and the Vulga.[1]

Built in 1903, named after Themis, Goddess of Justice, and with a crew of 19, she had a maximum speed of 8.9 knots and her normal cargo was iron ore from the Nova Scotia Steel and Coal Company (NSSCC) to Europe.[2] The choice of name was an interesting one in what Themis represented. In the Greek pantheon Themis was a Titaness, but not as modern representations have her. She was not blindfold, and carried no sword. She represented Justice, not by coercion, but by common consent- and she could see exactly what she was doing. Her particular cargo was destined to be offloaded onto the quayside at Rotterdam, then transferred by barge up the Rhine to Duisburg where it had been sold to three German steelmaking companies; Krupps, the Rheinishe Steelworks and the Phoenix Company. No greyhound, she was designed to plod her way with bulk cargo, to and fro across long distances under the command of Captain Gulliksen, who seems, to judge by later events, to have been a man with very much a mind of his own, steady, but perhaps lacking in a certain imagination, or patience.

None of the documentation carried by the ship signified where the cargo was destined, and she carried no radio, having been built before this innovation was installed in ships. As in previous centuries she relied on word of mouth from passing ships, from signals received from shore, and from telegrams received from vessels such as pilot boats. She nosed her way across the grey waters of the North Atlantic completely unaware that a cataclysm was about to break out in Europe and that she perhaps carried in her hold the fate of the British government and the shape of British politics to come.

5

The Divided House

The meeting of the British Cabinet at 3.15pm on Friday 24 July 1914, as the Themis began to cross the Atlantic, was one composed of weary men who had wrestled with the seemingly insoluble problem of Irish Home Rule for years. In the strict legal sense they had achieved what successive Liberal administrations had failed to do since 1886, and had brought Home Rule for Ireland into law. On 24 May the Government of Ireland Bill, having passed through the Commons for the third year in succession, could not be stopped by the House of Lords, now shorn of its veto by the Parliament Act of 1911. The Bill had gone to the King for signature, and all that remained to do now was the formal procedure of reading the new Act onto the Statute Book.

However, on 21 May when the Bill was introduced for its third reading, several MPs had put forward the idea of exempting Ulster from the new Act, at least for some years in order to avoid civil war in Ireland which now threatened to break out. The Ulster Volunteers of the Protestant North and the Irish Volunteers of the Catholic South were heavily armed, had been training, and were ready to fight and Civil War looked likely to break out at any time. The Prime Minister, HH Asquith, was anxious to avoid this conflict and possibly instigated the next move which was when King George V invited representatives from all parties to a conference at Buckingham Palace for discussions with himself in the chair; with him there the discussions would remain civil. This conference met from 21 July to 24 July 1914 and broke up with no agreement. Thus, the Cabinet meeting in the afternoon of 24 July was largely taken up in discussions about what to do next. The Irish talks had broken down largely over the question of where the border between northern and southern Ireland would be. Winston Churchill, perhaps lugubriously, described the Cabinet discussions as toiling round the muddy byways of Fermanagh and Tyrone.[3]

The melodrama of what happened next is well known; a knock at the door announced a messenger from the Foreign Office bringing a paper for Sir Edward Grey. Most ministers had had enough of wrangling and Churchill in particular was not listening when Grey began to read his note out aloud; it was the text of the Austrian ultimatum to Serbia, a document that Churchill described as being unlike any other document penned in modern times. Tired though they were, they began to listen, and as they did so Ireland faded out of their minds, and Europe began to come into focus.

Churchill, First Lord of the Admiralty, himself saw the danger as acute; the Grand Fleet, which was concentrated for a large scale military exercise was kept united for the next few days, ready to act as necessary. It was by no means certain that a crisis in the Balkans would lead inevitably to a general war in Europe. There had been several occasions during the time of the Liberal government since 1906 when Grey had been involved in crises which threatened the peace of the continent, but astute diplomacy and maneuvering had averted the threat; the two Moroccan Crises of 1905-6 and 1911, and the Balkan Crisis of 1908-9 had shown the value of talking a path out of difficulty. Now the Foreign Secretary set himself to find a bridge between the disputative powers, to confer and to find a way to avoid bloodshed. It must have been with a growing sense of disbelief over the next week that he watched his interventions come to nothing as Austria invaded Serbia, Russia mobilized, Germany mobilized and then France. Like a line of automated dominoes the great powers of Europe fell over into the pit of war.

Britain did not have to join in. Despite an entente with France since 1904, and Russia since 1907 it was the policy of both Conservative and Liberal parties to avoid getting involved in other peoples' wars; they were bad for business. Lord Salisbury had understood this, and it underpinned his policy of Splendid Isolationism. After his departure from office in 1902 the new Prime Minister, Arthur Balfour had set up the Committee for Imperial Defence (CID), whose brief was to examine all aspects of the defence of Britain and its empire. The outcome of this had been a realization that Britain was dangerously exposed and friendless in a world with many potentially hostile powers in it. To remedy the situation Britain had formed the Entente Cordiale with France and Russia, which had grown closer since its inception and even extended to joint military planning at a theoretical level - but, unlike the agreement signed with Japan in 1902, was not an alliance - Britain was not bound to go to war if France or Russia did.

There was a certain predictable inevitability about events at the beginning of August 1914, given that the Germans were well aware of France's Plan XVII. Aware of the overwhelming strength of the Franco-Russian alliance, German military planners wisely declined the French expectation to dash over the Franco-German border into a hail of fire in which they would suffer horrendous casualties. Instead they had come up with the Schlieffen plan whereby they intended to overwhelm the French quickly, as they had done in 1870, then turn to face the Russians with

France defeated in the rear, thus neatly avoiding the two front war they feared would crush them like a nut. As originally envisioned the German 'right hook' would smash through Holland and Belgium, neatly avoiding the formidable French fortified killing zones all along the Franco-German border. There was a danger that the British would object to this course of action, given their signature to the Treaty of London in 1839 and German recognition of it in 1871, but it was an old treaty and Britain's army was not of a scale to worry any of the large continental armies. Germany, with 2.4 million reservists need hardly worry about a nation that could muster, at most, about 200,000 trained men. The Austrian ultimatum to Serbia was followed by invasion; the Russians mobilized, the Germans followed suit, and the French, true to their treaty obligations to Russia did likewise. General war sparked off in Europe, and all that Sir Edward Grey could do to avert it ended in failure. Under no obligation to join in, the British government was nonetheless anxious to look after her interests, and it was most certainly not in those interests to have German dominance of Europe. It was also not tolerable to have the German fleet bombarding the French North coast whilst the British navy stood by; for a while it seemed that Britain might stay out of the war if the Germans guaranteed not to do this. However, it was the German request to Belgium to allow free passage of the German army to attack Northern France that changed the nature of the war for Britain. Belgium's King Albert informed the German Government that Belgium was not a public thoroughfare, and denied their request, whilst seeking assurances from Britain that they would honour their treaty obligations towards his country.

Certainly it was traditional British policy to work against foreign armies occupying the Low Countries. The Treaty of London of 1839 was to safeguard against such an event by guaranteeing the neutrality of Belgium, newly independent from Spain, and it had been signed by several European powers including Prussia, and reaffirmed in 1871 by the newly established German Empire. This old treaty placed the British government in a very difficult position. Firstly, there was no denying that Great Britain had signed this treaty. If she did not honour it, then her prestige and standing in the world would undoubtedly suffer. To a pragmatic observer it might have seemed that Britain's best course would have been to deny the obligation as one well past its sell-by date, applicable to a previous generation and not binding nearly 50 years after its last confirmation. That would not be an honourable thing to do, but it provided a face-saving way out of the mess if needed. Secondly, however, was the nature of the government facing the problem; they were Liberals, and the Liberal party was traditionally the home of anti-war sentiment. Why then should they go to war?

The nature of Liberalism is fluid and definition imprecise, but respect for the rule of law, change through reform and the manufacture of consensus are three factors strong in Liberal ideology. If Germany attacked Belgium then she outraged all three of these. Gladstone had been quite clear on this in 1870 when he warned France and Prussia not to violate Belgium in their war; he viewed the sacredness of Belgium's borders just as important as any other country's borders. The principle that it was not acceptable for large aggressive nations to attack and oppress their smaller neighbours was deeply engrained in Liberal thinking.

Insofar as a treaty was the nearest thing to international law that existed at the time, Germany was breaking an obligation undertaken by her own predecessor state which the new German Empire had recognized in 1871. In 1885 Bismarck had asked if Britain would fight in the event of Belgium being attacked and had been told that she would if she had an ally. In 1887 both France and Germany, at the point of conflict, sent Belgium messages that her neutrality would be respected; and Edward Grey himself had taken legal advice on Britain's obligation to Belgium if she was attacked and opinion was that Britain was obliged to assist. A consensus of powers had concerted to guarantee Belgian neutrality, and Germany had broken that consensus. Liberals sought to reform international relations through the manufacture of balance, but this did not mean tamely standing by and allowing other powers to do as they wished on the world stage. The Kaiser's policy of Weltpolitik, and the construction of its instrument, the High Seas Fleet, had left the British feeling threatened as to their position in the world and caused an arms race on the world's oceans in which Britain had taken a lead.

Asquith and Grey and some of their Cabinet were Liberal Imperialists, conscious of their duty to maintain Britain's power, prestige and preeminence in the world. To allow Germany to attack Belgium without consequence from Britain would be to threaten that pre-eminence. Nevertheless, as has been made perfectly clear by the recent publication of excerpts from Lewis Harcourt's diary, half of the Cabinet was determined to break the government up before it could commit the 'crime' of declaring war. The dissenters were Harcourt, McKinnon Wood, Morley, Simon, Pease, Burns, Lloyd George, Birrell, Samuel, Runciman, Beauchamp.[4]

They made it quite plain to Asquith that they were not prepared to go to war if Germany merely 'traversed' part of German territory. However they were clear among themselves that an occupation of Belgium as a whole would be regarded as a British interest. Lloyd George, as it later transpired, committed a gross breach of Cabinet confidentiality by telling George Riddell, Editor of *The News of the World*, on 2 August[5] that the government had agreed to remain neutral if the Germans undertook not to attack the coast of France or to enter the Channel to attack French Shipping.

The government teetered on the point of breaking up, and the interesting possibility of a coalition of Liberal Imperialists with Conservatives raised its head; the country had to be governed. The invasion of Belgium along all points of the frontier then swept most of the anti war camp's objections away and the government stayed intact, mostly as the country went towards war.

To make the position very clear to the Germans, the British government, upon hearing of the German invasion of Belgium on 3 August sent them an ultimatum to withdraw their troops or Britain would declare war on Germany. It was ignored, so on 4 August Britain found herself at war; only two Liberal ministers resigned, the septuagenarian John Morley who was a life long pacifist, and John Burns. Burns was a curious figure in the Cabinet; the first working class man to be a member of the executive, he saw the war rather as a plot by capitalists to enslave the people he called 'Industrials' and his resignation was principled if somewhat confused. This impression of confusion emanates from his helpfulness in the next few months in proposing measures to his ex colleagues to aid recruiting, so he may have had second thoughts about his principles. David Lloyd George, Chancellor of the Exchequer, appeared to consider resignation, but considering his belligerent stance towards Germany in the Moroccan Crisis of 1911 the question hovers over how much of his threat was political posturing; at any rate he did not resign. The Government took Britain to war - and their lately bitter opponents supported what they did.

Given the bitterness of the strife between the Conservatives and the Liberals over Ireland, it is remarkable how quickly they buried their differences. Apocryphally at the suggestion of the King the parties agreed to bury the hatchet in the face of an external threat so Bonar Law, the Conservative leader, had written to Asquith on 2 August on behalf of his party opining that it would be fatal to the honour and security of the United

Kingdom if they hesitated to support France and Russia, offering support to the government in any measures they considered necessary.[6] This support manifested itself almost immediately after the declaration of war in Asquith setting up the Parliamentary Recruiting Committee (PRC) in which the main parties pooled their efforts and expertise to encourage men to swell the army. That normal politics melted in the face of war was obvious from the example set by the French whose violently opposed factions set aside their differences on 28 August to form a National Government, the *Union Sacree* under Viviani, which could fight the war as a nation united. This example cannot have been lost upon the British Prime Minister.

That Asquith did not like coalitions is well known. However, just because one does not like something does not mean that one will not do it if necessary, and Asquith was, if nothing else, a pragmatist. Indeed he had to be or he could not have presided over a Cabinet of such talent as he did, so varied and assertive as it was, full of strong minds and ideas. He was certainly no ideologue or he could not have survived.

Asquith was able to take advantage of the new Ecumenicism among politicians to step down from his second Cabinet job, that of Secretary of War; he had been moonlighting at this task after the resignation of Col. Jack Seeley earlier in the year after the 'Curragh Mutiny' in Ireland. Following his usual practice of appointing the best qualified person he could find to do a job, the Prime Minister hit on Herbert Kitchener as Britain's number one military expert. Kitchener of Khartoum had achieved almost godlike status with the British public following his performances in the empire's war, and at the beginning of August was in the UK on leave from his job as Commander in Chief of the Egyptian Army. It is possible that he got wind of what he was about to be offered and did not particularly want it, not being a politician by nature. He entrained for Dover and boarded the cross channel ferry, but Asquith sent a messenger after him and he was compelled to accompany Asquith's Mercury back to Downing Street. It was rumoured that Kitchener was a Tory but Asquith had no compunctions about placing men from other parties into positions of power - he placed FE Smith, a leading Conservative in charge of the newly formed Press Bureau, on Kitchener's recommendation, to control what the newspapers said. To CP Scott, writing to John Dillon, the Irish Nationalist MP on 9 August, all this was significant:

'We have, I think, no longer a Liberal government... and to all intents and purposes there is a Coalition, the first symbols of which are the

appointments of Lord Kitchener as a member of the Cabinet and (a minor matter) of FE Smith as press-correspondent .... This state of things if likely to continue and develop and will have tremendous reactions on our politics....[7]

It took Asquith some time to persuade him, but one of his great strengths as Prime Minister was that he was very, very persuasive; Kitchener eventually accepted the post, and shortly after that attended his first Cabinet meeting where he informed the incredulous government that the war would take at least 4 years and that they would have to field armies of millions.[8] Sir Edward Grey spoke afterwards of a stunned silence in the Cabinet but coming from the mouth that it did, they could hardly gainsay it. It was the appointment of Kitchener that shaped the form which Britain's intervention was to take.

As a young officer Kitchener had observed the performance of French Territorial troops in the Franco Prussian war and he had formed a low opinion of them. The Haldane army reforms in the early years of the Liberal government had rationalized and made more efficient the defence of Britain and she had two small armies which could muster about 100,000 men in each; the Regular Army, and the Territorial Army which was for Home Service and composed of part time troops and reservists. The Regular army, schooled by hard experience in the Boer War, was excellent. The Territorials however were untried and Kitchener did not trust them any more than the French Territorials he had seen break and run from the Prussians in 1870. This was unfortunate because the British Territorials were in fact far better trained and equipped than the French troops of the 1870s with a similar name; the only real resemblance was the name. He did not wish to dilute the quality of the Regular Army by huge influxes of new recruits so determined to set up new armies altogether from scratch. By 1916 there were to be 6 new army groups now known as K1-K6 and numbering over 2 million men. In August 1914 there was no question of how men were to be got - they would volunteer and be encouraged to do so.

For some years Lord Roberts, legendary general of Empire, had been the enthusiastic head of a pressure group known as the National Service League (NSL) which was agitating for peacetime conscription on the continental pattern. It was, he argued, the only way to defend the empire efficiently. Nonetheless, this was seen by the leadership of the parties as being politically undesirable because it was not the 'British' way of doing things and the electorate would never accept it. That was probably true.

12

Others wished to see Cadet training on a compulsory basis in schools so that gradually a group of young men would emerge who were at least familiar with the rudiments of soldiering - but it came to nothing, despite the proliferation of quasi military groups for boys such as the Scouts, the Boys Brigade and the Church Lads. Kitchener's new armies would be found from volunteers.

It is difficult to know what was in Asquith's mind at this time perhaps because of his burning of most of his own papers in a bonfire later in his life. However he was in the habit of writing letters to a young woman, Venetia Stanley, sometimes several times a day telling his thoughts to her; or at least some of them. On 31 October 1914 he informed her that he had burned most of the letters he had received in his life:

'...not without a malicious complacency at the disservice I am doing to any biographer who may be foolish enough hereafter, to take me in hand'.[9]

Penetrating any rationale behind this thinking takes one into the realms of speculation. Asquith's psychological make-up was perhaps odd by the standards of today - or perhaps not. It might be odder to think that his Cabinet contained a man with a collection of child pornography, a man who had consented to sexual abstinence with his wife on their honeymoon night, and a man who had a mistress that everyone knew of, yet did not talk about. Intimate relations with Asquith's wife had ceased several years before after a warning that another pregnancy would kill her. It is clear from more than one account that he drank too much on occasion, being very fond of brandy and champagne. This of itself was not unusual in men of his generation where 'units' were a concept unknown, and over-consumption the rule rather than the exception. He was on occasion to be seen rather the worse for wear in Parliament, but he was not alone in this either; Churchill was similarly disposed as were others. Nonetheless before the war he was not generally referred to as "Squiff" save among his deepest enemies and drinking off the stress of office did not seem to impair his judgment. His political enemies may have exaggerated the extent of his addiction to drink above the norm of his peers. Indeed, it may not have been drink at all that earned him his nickname. He was a heavy man who moved slowly, and when he turned to look at something he turned his whole body, not just his head. Lord Beaverbrook, no political friend of his described him thus:

'Asquith had a shuffling gait. As he walked he extended his right hand in front of him as if he wished to ward off unseen obstacles. This mannerism gave the impression to strangers and to those who were unfamiliar with his private life that he was given to excessive drinking and insobriety. I do not deny that I have seen him on occasions while he was under the influence of the champagne he had consumed, but such a condition was unusual and infrequently observed, even by his closest associates.' [10]

The previous Prime Minister, Henry Campbell Bannerman had dubbed him 'The Sledgehammer' for the strength of his logic, clarity of speech, and sheer ability to flatten his opponents in debate, and that was his nickname in the House.

His occasional groping of young women, shocking by the standards of today, was accepted among those who knew him and shrugged off as being a small detail in his character. Ottoline Morrell, who was a friend of Asquith when she was 25 and he 45, fled from him when he attempted to pounce on her in 1898; but in later years renewed her friendship with him and his family. The composer Ethel Smyth, a suffragist angry at Asquith's refusal to support votes for women, wrote:

'I think it is disgraceful that millions of women should be trampled underfoot because of the convictions of an old man who notoriously can't be left alone in a room with a young girl after dinner.' [11]

With social attitudes towards women as they were then this is perhaps not surprising - Asquith was a product of the Victorian age. However, usefully, whether or not his relations with Venetia Stanley were sexual or not, he seems to have felt the need always for a young female muse and whatever else it may have done, has done some favours for history because he liked to write to them. Venetia Stanley was the most intense and the one who received most of his letters; he also liked to pick her up in his chauffeur driven car and go for drives out into the country with her on Friday afternoons; and she went willingly enough it seems, week after week and month after month. He did not tell her everything, but his letters to her provide perhaps the clearest light on a period of history that, considering it is so recent, remains relatively opaque. He was often indiscreet with her, giving her letters, information and telegrams, along with military secrets, but the deep workings of his own mind remain unclear. He told her so much, but left such a lot out; his own comments on what he was trying to bring about would be invaluable; but for the most part they are not there. Certainly it is a reasonable censure on him that he was, on occasion, writing to her during meetings of the Cabinet when he should have been paying attention when major strategy was being decided.

It would be too much of an assumption to see Asquith's relationship with Venetia as a sexual one. Apart from the disparity in age (he was in his sixties, she 28) there is more of the tone of idealization in the way he wrote to her - more of the 'courtly love' of the Middle Ages than of lust. His wife Margot knew all about it, and in response to her voiced concern he told her that Venetia was no threat to her. It appears that Asquith had to be 'in love' - to feel that frisson and enthusiasm all the time; Venetia was the most intense of his 'amours' but she was not the last. Any doubts on this may be dispelled by a letter from Edwin Montague, the young new Cabinet Minister in his 30s, whom Venetia eventually married, to her on 3 April 1915, speaking of his boss and his fiancée:

'I want him to have fun – no fun can be like being with you - **but can a lover who means business put up with it?**[12]

The clear implication that Asquith does not mean business in the 'lover' way may exonerate him somewhat of sexual infidelities.

On 8 September 1914 he wrote to Venetia that Kitchener had said he would have 50 divisions in 6 months, just over a million men. This casual mentioning of state secrets was a habit he continued with his next 'muse', Mrs Sylvia Henley, and he was very free with facts. However, as to the inner workings of his own mind; his schemes, his plans, his hopes and especially his opinions on his colleagues and their doings; they remain an enigma, but with an occasional insight. His brief musing over whether or not to send Jack Pease to be Irish Secretary on the grounds that a clever man was not needed there at this time is a good example of what he really thought of one of his colleagues. It would be most illuminating to know much more of what he thought of his other colleagues; what he thought of their schemes and plans, machinations, wheelings and dealings, but we do not. Particularly, he seems to have been well aware of plots against him, and able to take measures to address any conspiracies that threatened to unseat him, but to Venetia, he never commented on such things. What he really thought of Kitchener, Lloyd George, Churchill and especially Bonar Law, remains a mystery, illuminated only by the occasional passing remark in conversation or a letter.

The first patriotic flush of war buried party enmity for a few short weeks. Indeed if anything it seemed to have firmed up Asquith's control of the Commons, as many more Tory MPs than Liberal were army officers and they left to join their units. Commencing on 9 August the bulk of the British Expeditionary Force (BEF) were in France within two weeks of the Declaration of war and the whole affair was handled with smoothness and efficiency following plans worked out years before. Grouping near Boulogne, they began to advance towards the Belgian frontier and reached Mons by 22 August. There they opened fire on the advancing Germans and began to take casualties.

The Nation in Arms

Given that the effective British force in the field was about 80,000 men, tiny in the face of the German forces, these casualties would have to be replaced as soon as possible. On the day that he took over at the War Office, 5 August, Kitchener issued orders for the expansion of the Army. On 6 August Parliament sanctioned the raising and funding of 500,000 men and on 11 August 'YOUR KING AND COUNTRY NEED YOU: A CALL TO ARMS' was published by the War Office asking for the first 100,000 men. Yet it was quite clear that the flow of volunteers would need to be sustained and that measures needed to be taken to keep them coming.

The Parliamentary Recruiting Committee (PRC) was set up, by Asquith according to the Times, and contained a cross party membership whose brief was to recruit the new forces. Its brief was clear enough and the task was to be carried out mainly through posters and regional recruiting offices. Although it stayed in existence until October 1915, then re-constituted under Lord Derby until 20 July 1916, it held only one full meeting attended by all, which was on 31 August 1914. Nine of the members were Liberals led by their Chief Whip Percy Illingworth; six were Conservatives led by Arthur Steel-Maitland, their party Chairman. Sir Jesse Herbert, (Lib) suggested that if recruitment were to be efficient then some sort of household return might be useful to find out how many potential recruits there actually were. The Liberals were discussing the possibility among themselves of compulsory military service. According to Harcourt, Churchill raised it as a possibility in Cabinet on 25 August. Lord Emmott, the First Commissioner of Works thought Churchill's statement an atrocious waste of time.[13] Jack Pease, the President of the Board of Education said that Churchill harangued them on the necessity for

Compulsory Service for half an hour and bored them. Lloyd George said the people would not listen to such proposals, whilst Asquith said it would divide the country from one end to the other.[14] Charles Hobhouse said that most of the Cabinet did not wish to speak of it, but Churchill insisted on doing so, saying that if they did not speak of it now then they never would. Kitchener said it might come to it later, but he would make no appeal for it now. Harcourt noted that the PM dismissed it as being among the 'remote possibilities' they faced; he did not even mention it in his customary letter to the King on Cabinet proceedings. [15]

Some Conservatives were not happy with the idea of compulsion, Steel-Maitland stating that it was too inquisitorial and was probably not the best way of getting men anyway. Nor was he alone; LS Amery, a military minded Liberal Unionist MP wrote to Bonar Law on 26 August suggesting that a recruiting scheme could be set up across the country through the party organisations already existing in towns, counties and villages, but ended:

'We are bound to do what we can with the existing system until Kitchener himself asks for compulsion.'[16]

There is a delicious irony to this in view of later developments. The PRC decided by a majority that registration forms would be sent anyway to gain some idea of who was available for military service and who was doing what jobs, and this was done on 12 November 1914, but there was no legal obligation to fill the forms out. 4,400,000 circulars were sent out with the aid of the Local Government Board and party local organizations, 2,250,000 replies received and 225,000 promises of enlistment made. The information was sent to officers commanding regional depots, to be compiled into registers. The whole scheme was carried out by some 2,000 volunteers over a period of a few months, so its activities were rather sporadic as to area and haphazard in method, and the end results less than conclusive - or useful.

The men in power were creatures of their time and well knew that conscription was contrary to British traditions - but there was the consideration of organized Labour. The pre-war years had been plagued by widespread industrial unrest, and indeed the Triple Alliance of Coalminers, Railwaymen and Transport workers had a national strike planned for October 1914, which the war averted. An attempt to impose compulsion on British workers at this date, workers who were very suspicious of any attempt to regiment and chain the working classes, would probably have been met with serious unrest. This was very well illustrated in a letter from Robert Williams, Secretary of the National Transport Workers' Federation to Ramsay McDonald on 6 August:

'We ought to be fully prepared to counter the machinations of the yellow Press with defiant working class pronouncements. Personally, if I am compelled to shoot, I would much prefer to blaze away at the enemies I know inside our own country than attempt to murder member of my own class at the behest of blood drunken maniacs like Churchill and others. We must be prepared to organize forcible revolt against conscription, come in whatever form it may.' [17]

The clerk to the PRC was Richard Humphrey Davies who in presenting the minutes of the PRC to the British Library in 1967 wrote:

'...throughout its proceedings, the Committee worked in the greatest harmony, taking care, at the same time, that it was a voluntary effort to secure recruits...From the beginning to the end the Committee acted in perfect friendship, each member recognizing that the other were doing their best to make the common cause victorious...Its work... was a striking manifestation of British unity in the face of great peril.' [18]

Clearly, in some matters, inter party cooperation continued, no matter what overall relations were like.

The magazine *London Opinion* had hailed the appointment of Kitchener as Secretary of War on the front cover of its 5 September issue with an image of him pointing out at the reader, drawn by Alfred Leete. This was so striking that the PRC asked permission to use it as their first poster and it became the fore-runner of a plethora of recruiting posters for the next almost two years until they became unnecessary. Contrary to myth it was not this poster that sparked the rush of men to the colours at the beginning of the war; the initial 100,000 new recruits had joined up within 3 weeks, before the poster came out. In the wave of enthusiasm that swept the nation it was only reasonable to applaud their patriotism and no-one really gave much thought to how the process was being carried out. As men with no uniforms or rifles drilled in playgrounds or fields you might have noticed that your bus was running late, or that there were fewer of them, but this was perhaps to be expected in time of war. The whole thing had happened rather too quickly for anyone to give serious thought to anything other than the fact that the army needed men. Beyond that other things paled into insignificance. The Admiralty did see that if too many of their shore workers joined up then they would not be able to keep their ships running so they issued Admiralty badges for men to wear on their arms to impress upon them that they were doing vital war work. Some firms began to ask for these badges to stop their employees from being pestered by recruiters on the street who would ask them why they were still not in uniform. But the expectation of a short war and the almost complete unpreparedness for a long one lulled most people into thinking that no sorting out of workers was needed. Vital machinists, engineers and metallurgists flocked to join up in a rush that put factories into chaos as workers disappeared into the ranks, buses not to run because there were no crews, and less coal to be produced because the miners had gone. In a sort of glorious British muddle the men of Britain swarmed into uniform, and the Ship of State sailed on. The shipment of iron however, had sailed into even more dangerous waters. [19]

Chapter 2

All at Sea

The SS Themis with her fateful cargo was steaming up the English Channel just as war was about to break out. As she proceeded up the shipping lanes she came into sight of the lighthouse at Dungeness. Mr George Stout, ship-broker of Glasgow, acting as charter agent for the Nova Scotia Steel and Coal Company (NSSCC), the owner of the ore and charterer of the Themis had telephoned Lloyds of London on 3 August asking them to have the Dungeness signal station order the Themis to stop and await further orders. Stout had already signaled to another ship whose charter he was handling, the Vulga, also loaded with iron ore, to divert to Middlesborough, and this was done. Late on 3 August Stout received a message from Lloyds saying that the Themis had received the signal and was hove to off Dungeness awaiting instructions.[1]

Yet later he received a second telegram stating that the Themis had passed Dungeness heading east and had failed orders. The signal station at Dungeness reported, upon inquiry, that the Themis had received their signals. Captain Gulliksen, after a few hours of waiting at Dungeness, asked the signal station from whom the order came, and upon being told the Charterers, he had replied that his orders were for Rotterdam and that there must be a mistake. He then asked whose signature was on the order and was told that there was none. A second telegram from the signal station said that the Themis had waited several hours during the night, but had then sailed on without further communication.

An urgent telegram was then sent to Dover that the signal station hoist the SUT signal which stood for 'wait here for orders' and this was done. The Themis made no acknowledgement of the signal as she passed Dover and sailed on easterly, presumably heading for Rotterdam. It is possible that the Captain and crew simply wished, after a long voyage, to get home. However, Lloyds informed Mr Stout that there had been a heavy rainstorm and that it was possible that the Themis had not seen the signal flags.

By early Wednesday 5 August the Themis was in the Straits of Dover. At three o' clock in the morning she was seen some miles off Deal by HMS Falcon, a destroyer, part of the Dover Patrol, detailed to intercept and board all vessels sighted travelling the Channel from a westerly direction. The

First World War was four hours old. Presumably she was spot-lit by the warship and told to stop for inspection.

In response to this signal the Themis heaved to and a boat was detailed to board her under the command of Gunner Ernest Smith whom Captain Wauton of the Falcon instructed to search and examine her papers. A Gunner in the Navy was a Warrant Officer's post and a small TBD (destroyer) like Falcon did not carry many commissioned officers. Captain Wauton's title was a courtesy as he was a 29 year old Lieutenant and had commanded Falcon since 1912. It was a routine matter and the ship made no demur when signalled, so the boarding boat only contained 4 men, of whom Smith was the senior - they quickly crossed the dark gap between the vessels, the sea being calm. Even had Gulliksen wished not to stop, he had no choice. The Falcon, a turtle decked destroyer built in the Govan Yard in 1899, could do 30 knots and could literally sail circles round the Themis. Smith saw from the ship's papers that she was registered in Norway and was thus a neutral, and was headed for Rotterdam in another neutral country. Her crew was in fact Dutch and the Captain Norwegian. The forwarding agents for the cargo, responsible for freighting it to Rotterdam was a steel trading company called Jacks & Co of Glasgow. There was, on the face of it, no reason to delay her further and after hailing his Captain to confirm this, Smith signed a certificate of clearance allowing the Themis to proceed up the Channel. Smith was aware, as he stated later, that there were no steelworks in Holland, but iron ore was not contraband and could be going on anywhere from Holland. It was permissible cargo on a neutral ship and his duty, by the book, was to let it through. [2]

Mr Wilson, one of the Jacks & Co Directors had indicated in a phone call to Mr Stout that it was desirable that the ship did not go to Rotterdam, but Mr Van Uden, forwarding agent in Rotterdam later telegrammed that the Captain had disobeyed his orders received at Dungeness because the message he received was unsigned. Messrs Jacks & co were very anxious it seemed at this time, that the cargo did not reach Rotterdam. When pressed as to whose responsibility it was that the ship went on its way, Mr Stout was very firm in his view that it was none other than the Captain of the Themis. The owners of the vessel in Norway had received a telegram from Jacks & Co, ordering that the vessel should actually proceed to Greenock where in fact arrangements were made for her to dock. [3]

Early on the morning of Thursday 6 August the Themis arrived at Hook of Holland where Captain Gulliksen was interviewed by Van Uden's representatives who came out in the pilot boat, and was told to proceed to Greenock. The Captain replied that he was not insured for the risk of being at sea during war; it was not safe to lie at Hook of Holland, and he wished to dock his ship. On Friday 7 August he did in fact proceed up to Rotterdam and began to discharge his cargo. Seven thousand tons of iron ore were discharged onto the quay before Mr Stout was aware of it, and before Jacks & Co were aware of it. Mr Stout was of opinion that he could have done nothing else to stop this. Since Captain Gulliksen did not have control over shore facilities the unloading can only have been carried out with the assistance of Messrs Van Uden, forwarding agents for NSSCC. [4]

At this point a few hundred tons of iron ore remained on the ship that needed to be emptied. This was soon done, and the Captain handed over his bills of lading. On 5 August King George V had issued a proclamation against trading with the enemy. On 8 August the Trading with the Enemy Act came into force. The ore was taking up quayside space and needed to be moved; but to where? Control of this lay with Van Udens who were in turn agents of the forwarding company, Jacks & Co of Glasgow. This was later disputed, a case being made that Van Udens were never agents for Jacks & Co, but for the NSSCC. Jacks & Co were in fact the principle forwarding agents, ultimately responsible for handling the payments made for the ore. The position occupied by the ore from now on would to some extent, and arguably, determine the future governance of the United Kingdom.

Building a Consensus

The Prime Minister meanwhile was wrestling with a problem he could well have done without. Until 4 August the matter dominating British politics had been the vexed one of the Irish question. Theoretically the issue was done and dusted. On 25 May the Government of Ireland Act had passed the Commons, was rejected by the Lords, but having been rejected twice before, the Parliament Act of 1911 came into force and the new law received the Royal assent shortly afterwards. The anger of the Unionists in Northern Ireland was put into abeyance by a government Bill amending the new Act which proposed that Ulster be temporarily excluded from the Home Rule settlement.

John Redmond, the Irish Nationalist leader, naturally wished the Home Rule government to be set in place as soon as possible. When the war broke out he did not sign the inter-party truce, hoping that Asquith would understand why he could not, but gave him a verbal assurance of his support. Asquith's government depended on Nationalist support, and he needed to deliver something to the Nationalists or he would no longer be Prime Minister. An added complication was that it was plain that many Irish would not feel inclined to volunteer to fight Germany if Home Rule was withheld. On the other hand if he set up Home Rule in Ireland without an amending act excluding Ulster then he would face a rebellion in the North. He would also lose the support of the Conservatives. His clear priority was to preserve National Unity, as was Bonar Law's. The Prime Minister wrote to Bonar Law on 8 August:

'I am, as I know you are, anxious above all things, that in the circumstances which surround us, no impression shall be given to the world that we are, any of us, intent on the pursuit of domestic controversy.'[5]

In this he was completely accurate; Bonar Law was indeed anxious not to do anything that would impair the British war effort against Germany, and this was the position he clung to until the following May. Asquith's belief in Bonar Law's patriotism and desire to maintain National Unity was not misplaced. The solution Asquith decided on was logical in a clumsy, eloquent and incongruous sort of way and he did it in close consultation with Redmond and Dillon, the Irish Nationalist leaders. In his mind also may have been the fact that not only would his government fall without the Irish, but that failure to deliver Home Rule would undermine Redmond, leaving the way open for far less moderate men to assume leadership of Irish Nationalism. He hoped that the majority of reasonable Unionists would go along with his actions, and thought their leaders would confine themselves to verbal protests.

Austen Chamberlain, leader of the Liberal Unionists, who had merged with the Conservatives as one party organisation finally in 1912, was unhappy with the idea that the Home Rule Law should become statute, wishing to amend it and guarantee that Ulster would not be part of it; Churchill told him that there as no practical difference between what he proposed and what the Liberals proposed except that the Liberal course of action avoided a quarrel with the Irish people.

Asquith knew that to the Irish Nationalists, upon who his support depended, the placing of the Home Rule Act on the Statute Book was an action of deep significance and that unless he did so, their support could not be taken for granted. In similar fashion the controversial Act which disestablished the Church in Wales had to go through the same process or he risked alienating much nonconformist Liberal support in Wales. He had little choice in that both of these things had to be done in order to avoid dire consequences.

The Conservatives were attempting to bring in their own bill suspending all legislation until the close of the war or of this Parliament in 1915, but their course of action would mean that Home Rule and Welsh disestablishment would not actually become law. In practice this would mean the end of the government as the Irish withdrew support. There would also be great anger in Wales and perhaps a schism amongst Liberals.

It is quite clear that Asquith was determined to preserve unity of purpose in Westminster if he could, and, caught between a rock and a hard place, he was banking on intelligence he had received that the Conservatives were not united on what to do over either Ireland or the Welsh church. In this purpose he had a very important ally, King George V who wrote to him on 25 August:

'My Dear Prime Minister, In this exceptionally anxious time it is really too sad to think that we are threatened with a revival of party strife with regard to Ireland. As you told me you find it impossible to postpone the question until after the war, I am only too anxious to do anything in my power to help you secure an agreement. I have therefore written the enclosed letter which you are at liberty to make such use of as you may see fit, even to its publication. You may consider such a course to be unusual, but the existing circumstances are unprecedented.[6]

The letter called for: *'forbearance and generous concessions on the part of the responsible leaders, supported by those whom they represent.'*

Asquith showed this letter to Redmond, Sir Edward Carson the Ulster Unionist leader, and Bonar Law on 25 August. The idea of royal displeasure at any display of disunity, and even more the notion of the letter being published, probably focused their minds well. There was, at this time, no break in the show of National Unity. Such was the outward appearance of common purpose and unity in August that the Editor of the *Manchester Guardian*, CP Scott wrote in his diary:

'Coalition government might be announced.'[7]

and to Leonard Hobhouse, Liberal philosopher and writer later in the month:

'No chance I hope yet of universal military service. At least the Morning Post yesterday said that at present it would be useless because our organization couldn't cope with it, but if the war goes on long no doubt some form of compulsory training will be proposed, and whatever is proposed by the government would, under existing conditions, be adopted. We have already what is virtually a Coalition government and it seems to me that in some ways it would be better to have one that was avowedly such. It might help towards greater independence and cooperation of Radicalism and Labour'.[8]

Asquith was actually having some success in finding an accommodation, as a letter from James Hope MP, the Conservative member for Sheffield Central on 1 September to Lord Edmund Talbot the Conservative Chief Whip in the Commons, made very clear:

'They - that is the people who control the government - would jump at a chance of dropping the Amending Bill - and if we cannot get a tolerable settlement we must at least have that Bill... the extent and violence of the feeling shown points to a greater breach between the govt and their Jacobin supporters than I had supposed; and I cannot help thinking that we may have to revise our ideas about not joining them in a formal Coalition.[9]

Talbot did not agree with him but it is very useful in pinpointing that the notion of coalition at the beginning of the war was far from unpalatable to both the editor of the main Liberal newspaper and an influential Conservative Member of Parliament. The idea was abroad and being talked about.

John W Hills, Conservative MP for Ludlow wrote to Bonar Law on 6 September stating:

'It seems to me that we as a party, and Ulster have to make a big sacrifice in order to secure unity in the face of the enemy. It may be that the government are unreasonable and unfair in what they are doing ... Our national existence, and indeed European civilisation, are at stake; any hint of disunion at home would directly hinder us in the fight....'[10]

It is hard to imagine the disruption that would have followed a collapse of the government at this time. Coalition was in the air though, Churchill writing to Lord Robert Cecil on 8 September:

'No-one can tell from week to week what the course of the war will be, or what political combinations may be necessary to secure its effective conclusion. No-one can foresee the shape in which the political parties will emerge from the struggle.' [11]

That the notion of coalition was possible must have been obvious when the two main parties held a joint meeting at the Guildhall on the morning of 4 September where Asquith, Bonar Law and Balfour shared the platform and the two party leaders spoke of why the war had begun, stressed the need for unity and quite clearly were united in their purpose of winning the war. On 9 September the right wing *Morning Post* hailed Asquith's speech:

'No finer appeal has ever been made to the British Nation. The Nation will respond to the call of its leader.'

Whilst the *Manchester Guardian* stated that: *'The Premier was impressive, as always'.* [12]

According to Leonard Mosley there was at least one leading Conservative who would have jumped at the chance to do something towards the war effort, and that was Lord Curzon:

'Without telling anyone in the Conservative Party he wrote a letter to the Prime Minister HH Asquith, offering his services. Asquith not only turned him down, but slyly let it be known that once more, Curzon was secretly planning to betray a pledge to his Party. Mortified, as well as rebuffed, the ex Viceroy wrote bitterly; 'Pitiful that at 39 one was thought fit to rule 300 millions of people, and at 55 is not wanted to do anything in an emergency in which our whole national existence is at stake'. [13]

However, any notions of formal coalition, whatever personal coalitions may be made, would have to first leap over the Irish Home Rule hurdle.

On 14 September Asquith told Venetia Stanley that it would be a really big thing if he could get Home Rule on the statute book after 3 years of ceaseless conflict and worry, and he felt that the Tories had a grievance that they could not parade. He clearly was gambling that the Tories would

26

be restrained by patriotic necessity from making a fuss and determined to use all his powers to get the matter of Ireland and Wales settled and done with.

The Defence of the Realm Act had passed into law very quickly by 8 August, giving the government emergency powers to fight the war. These included the power to pass secondary legislation by Order in Council, shortcutting the need for Parliamentary process. On 14 September an Order in Council was made suspending the Government of Ireland Act for six months, and the new and controversial Disestablishment of the Welsh Church until the end of the war. Effectively this placed the Acts on the statute book, the formal last process of a new law. It only remained to announce it in the House. The amending Act excluding Ulster would also have to wait, but the Irish had their parliament, even if they had to wait for it. That secured the government from falling. Asquith stood in the Commons to announce all this on 15 September and to temper it by stating that he would bring in an amending Bill for Ireland before the acts went into operation.

When he had finished speaking Bonar Law made a bitter speech in reply, and when he had finished the entire Unionist Party stood and walked out, as Asquith jokingly said afterwards, trying very hard to look like revolutionaries.

He made light of it, but it was no joke; and he had underestimated clearly what their reaction would be. No doubt it was a political mistake on his part, but it is hard to see what else he could have done. A great gulf had opened up between the Government and the Opposition. Bonar Law had compared Asquith to the Kaiser as a liar and a cheat and feelings ran equally high on the government side as ministers left the House in order not to resort to violence, Reginald McKenna having to lie down on a couch to recover from the urge to punch Bonar Law. The Conservative and Unionist Party now adopted a line of non cooperation; although hostility was temporarily masked by the proroguing of Parliament on Friday 18 September, the Liberals would have to run the war on their own, for now. Parliament did not reopen until 11 November. It only sat 12 times in November before recessing until 6 January 1915. From now until May 1915 Bonar Law's stated policy was to not obstruct the efficient running of the war, but also not to cooperate with the Liberals – not 'active opposition' but 'patriotic opposition'.

Thus, opportunities for open breaches were few, but the fury of the Conservatives is quite clear in this letter to Bonar law on 19 September from John Baird, Conservative MP for Glasgow Central, his Parliamentary Private Secretary, who was then serving in France:

'... Today's papers give an account of the Radical government's crowning rascality. It is impossible to put oneself in the frame of mind of people who are capable of such villainy....' [14]

There had been a certain anxiety among MPs that they were being detained in London when they could be of much more use in their constituencies organizing such things as recruiting, but there was also a certain amount of unreality to the air. The notion was still around that the war would be short, that the British could expect the French to do most of the fighting on land, and that the whole thing might be over by Christmas. Without this sense of slight detachment it would make little sense for the Parliament of a country at war to suspend its sittings for over a month at the very onset of a great national struggle, but Asquith perhaps took his sense of delegation too far. The Cabinet met daily until Wednesday 23 September, but thereafter they did not; they met when the Prime Minister called them, which was normally about three times a week. The individual ministers were left to run their own departments and there was no administrative body to maintain an overall control of what was done - the War Council was not instituted until late November. Asquith's style of government was to put a man in charge of a department and back him to the hilt; his loyalty to his colleagues was well known. This would have been well had the arrangement been reciprocal, but the absence of close control led in effect to his creations being satrapies and power bases for ambitious men to intrigue from. It also meant that cooperation between departments depended too much on personalities and the willingness to compromise, which was not always there. The Prime Minister spent much of his time in holding the balance between his ministers as they warred with each other - and against himself. More frequent Cabinet meetings or an effective War Council might have brought about a stronger and more collective notion of governance.

Asquith's conception of his own job as Premier was not as 'presidential' as Prime Ministers these days are expected to be. He saw himself as first among equals, and having entrusted a man to do a job, he saw it as his role to act as the balance between competing Ministers. Policy would emerge from the debate and struggles between his department heads,

28

and his job was to remain above it and keep the team pulling together. As he told Venetia on 29 December 1914:

'I suppose that as usual I shall have to try to compose the controversy- a storm in a slop bucket, if ever there was one...'[15]

Curiously this also explains his seeming lethargy as Prime Minister. If the work of government was being carried out by departments which were semi-independent, then he as Prime Minister was the overseer of the whole machine, and since he only had to step in when needed this left him time to play bridge, golf, drive out with Venetia - and write letters during Cabinet meetings. His appearance of lethargy disguising great activity was, he told Venetia, quite deliberate, and certainly he was capable of great energy when it was demanded. His reorganizing of the War Office at the beginning of November 1915 when Kitchener was in Gallipoli is a case in point, but it did lay him open to the charge of not taking much interest in the war, even to his contemporaries. He was most amused on 24 January 1915 when Lady Tree asked him 'with much apparent naïveté' if he took an interest in the war and praised her sense of humour to Venetia.[16] This has, nonetheless been much used against him. Ultimately it might be said that he was adequate, indeed excellent as a Prime Minister, but that the way he organized the administration of his government was a rationalized form of chaos. The man himself was sound, but the uncoordinated power struggle elevated to a form of government was not sound. Looking at his Cabinet, there was literally no-one else in a position strong enough to hold such a team together as long as he did; that was his achievement writ large, but efficient it was not.

Parliament had prorogued on Friday 18 September so the political bitterness following the Conservative walkout was not as overt as it might have been. FE Smith had only been in charge of the Press Bureau since 5 August but now resigned - ostensibly over such headlines as: *'Broken British regiments unable to stem German advance'* being allowed to appear on his watch, but the timing of it looks suspiciously as if he was following a party line. Asquith appointed the Solicitor General, Sir Stanley Buckmaster, to this task; and very well he did it too. Anything that appeared to threaten the good name or probity of the British Government was simply not allowed to appear, and he used his powers under the Defence of the Realm Act widely.

Asquith had famously said that coalitions hardly ever turn out well in our history, and it was known that he was not fond of the whole idea of coalition. Nonetheless, just because someone does not like an idea it does not mean that they will not act on it if it is necessary. The example of best practice was not too far away in the shape of

France who had formed a coalition almost as soon as war broke out, and, considering that National Unity is a prize asset to a nation at war, their move cannot have been lost on Asquith. His appointments of Kitchener, reputedly a Tory, and FE Smith, to positions of power and authority right at the outset indicate quite clearly that he was not averse to including members of the opposition in his government. It is also clear that Bonar Law's walkout had closed that door very firmly for the moment, at least as far as the Conservatives were concerned. However, the adjournment of the House until January meant that whatever happened in public life and in the conduct of the war happened outside the need to report to Parliament.

It might have been easier for the government, but discerning what actually happened becomes difficult because information and evidence has to be gleaned from the records of individual departments, diaries, letters and memoirs. Indeed, Asquith told Venetia on 20 September that it was a great relief to have the House not sitting because there were no answers to make to questions and no bores to suffer. Thus, there is surprisingly little on which to base any definite ideas on what might be about to happen and why it did happen.

Of course what would be infinitely easier than any other alternative would be a situation where the Nation as a whole was united with one government running its war effort - in the shape of a National government, or coalition. It appears not only that Asquith came to desire this as the most acceptable way forward, but that he made and signalled very obvious moves towards it over the next few months. It is possible, though not easy, to discern the Zeitgeist between the two opposing front benches changing between November 1914 and March 1915, until the idea of a coalition was very much on the table, and the only thing stopping it from happening was party politics. That the Conservatives wished to be involved in running the war, the greatest in British history, was natural. That many came to resent their own leaders holding them back from attacking the government was also natural. In the idea of 'patriotic opposition' there was a sort of moral high ground that would hold back some of the Conservative critics of the Liberal war effort - but only for so long until it began to chafe. If the

Conservative leaders resisted for long enough what their followers thought necessary to win the war, then they would inevitably face a challenge over their policies - and perhaps their leadership; they would lose control of their party. The issue around which the Conservatives who wanted active opposition coalesced, was that of compulsion as a more efficient way of organizing the nation's manpower.

Breaking the Impasse

On 12 October 1914 the first Battle of Ypres opened and it was to last a month during which the pre-war BEF took many casualties and had to throw every reserve it had into stopping the Germans from taking Ypres. The shaping and training of the new armies become more imperative with each passing day and the Prime Minister could not afford to have the opposition sulking on the sidelines. He did point up that there were penalties for such an action by ordering that Cabinet documents, normally circulated to the leaders of the opposition, should not be circulated, on the grounds of their inactivity, as it plainly did not concern them. The Conservatives were left to kick their heels, though as Asquith told Venetia, he did have some experience at building bridges over gaping chasms. This was rather how he saw his role too - as a great judge between his colleagues and an arbiter of the struggles between them. Unfortunately, at this time it looked as if the gulf between the government and the Conservatives could not be bridged. A foretaste of another great matter needing attention came on 29 October when a somewhat alarmed Kitchener told Asquith that the war was consuming seven times as much ammunition as any previous war and that if it continued, supply would not keep up with demand. He thought the war might end sooner than he anticipated because both sides would simply run out. The government had already taken steps to alleviate this problem by appointing a Shells Committee on 12 October under War Department auspices, which had increased the orders for ammunition and gun production. They had also expanded the number of firms contracted to supply the army and had underwritten the costs of expanding armaments works for companies who wished to do so. Since the British munitions industry was small, it appeared they had taken all the correct and needful steps. It is easy to claim, in retrospect, that not enough had been done, but in truth all concerned were facing a situation that was beyond their imaginations at any time before then. It is also worth considering that to some extent the government had never thought it would face a continental commitment on the scale that Kitchener was planning. If they had, then they would have prepared, as had other European powers, for a large army; but their notion had been that Britain's navy would do most of Britain's part in any war. Ammunition may not be conjured out of thin air, but the wand had been waved and orders were placed for what they thought was needed.

The problem for the Conservatives is that they were now effectively out of the loop as regards the running of the war. They had no access to the documents they needed if they were to give advice, if they were to criticize, or if they were to plan. True, their energies could be diverted into the war effort in a myriad of ways but their walkout meant that their hands no longer touched the levers of power. Yet this was a two edged weapon - if they were deprived, then so was Asquith; he needed a united nation which mobilized the talents, resources and energies of that part of the nation which the Conservatives represented. His moves to include Kitchener and FE Smith in running the war effort, and his formation of the cross party PRC may or may not have been tentative moves towards forming a coalition, but to some extent his inclination is irrelevant in the face of the stark fact that coalition was logical and desirable, and the need for it was becoming plainer as the war went on. Certainly at this time of the war Asquith seemed to people in all parties to give the nation the necessary leadership. In his speeches, his bearing, his conduct and manner in the house he seemed to be the great commander needed at the moment.

Cross party cooperation was in fact taking place as Labour's new leader Arthur Henderson did all that he could to assist the war effort. Henderson was as anti-war as Ramsay McDonald, who had resigned as leader in protest, but he reasoned that since there was a war, someone had to look after workers' interests, and that he was going to do the job properly. On 11 November Asquith paid special thanks to him in the Commons for the time and energy he was devoting to the war effort. In January 1915 Henderson accepted a post under the Home Office, offered by Herbert Samuel; he was made a Commissioner with the task of finding employment for Belgian refugees, which he carried out in partnership with the London Labour Councillor Susan Lawrence. In February he was joined by another Labour man, John Hodge, MP for Manchester Gorton, on another Committee to find work for disabled ex-servicemen. Later he was to help Lloyd George throughout the conferences with the Trades Unions, which led to the signing of the Treasury Agreement of March 1915, and then he served on Lloyd George's Munitions Committee. Although much criticized by some on the Labour left, Henderson had made a significant step forward, even a great triumph for his party in cooperating with Lloyd George; for the first time the Unions as a corporate body had spoken directly to government. There were advantages to cross party cooperation.

Asquith had not given up on drawing the Conservatives into closer cooperation either so in October he renewed an offer to Arthur Balfour that he rejoin the Committee on Imperial Defence (CID) and Balfour accepted, attending his first meeting on 7 October 1914.

Lloyd George also did something that was completely unthinkable unless he had Asquith's consent - he asked Austen Chamberlain to join him in private discussions at the Treasury on the details of his war budget. Chamberlain, who had been one of the contenders for the Conservative leadership in 1911, commanded the loyalty and support of the Unionist wing of the party (about half the MPs) and he accepted Lloyd George's invitation although he saw his position as rather anomalous:

'...I do not wish in the present grave crisis to refuse any assistance to the government which it is in my power to give and I am prepared therefore to accept your invitation and do my best to help you. If however I should find my situation an impossible one, you will, I hope, permit me to withdraw...' [17]

Apocryphally, Chamberlain was invited also to join the War Council but declined in deference to Bonar Law. Lloyd George also invited another prominent Conservative, Lord St Aldwyn, to sit in and advise on Treasury Committees, and he too accepted; Runciman at the Board of Trade found his input very useful. Asquith also invited Balfour, the ex-Conservative Prime Minister, to sit in on the meetings of his new War Council from the end of November 1914, and Balfour accepted this too. As Lord Beaverbrook later commented:

'...Balfour's cooperation with the government filled Bonar Law with a certain amount of anxiety. And he was right to be anxious'. [18]

Balfour, three years after his resignation as Conservative leader, was now back into active public life, and Bonar Law was concerned, feeling that his own position as leader was imperiled, his relations with Balfour being *'impersonal but impeccable correctitude'* - not that Balfour would be bothered by that.[19] Mr Walter Long, a leading Conservative, was also disturbed by this development and wrote to tell Bonar Law so, on 25 November.[20]

Balfour became very active indeed in carrying out tasks he was assigned - such as helping with coastal defences, urging the setting up of a large overseas base nearer Germany, and assisting in War Council deliberations about a war loan.

The Premier was determined, it seemed, to maintain national unity and to include the Conservatives in that, or at least those who wished to be included. Drawing up a list of new privy Councillors in December 1914 he was very disappointed by Lord Edward Talbot, the Conservative Chief Whip, refusing the honour as it destroyed the symmetry of his list, as he told Venetia, which would have been Talbot for the Tories, Arthur Henderson for the Labour Party and the Liberal Whip, Percy Illingworth, who had been working together in the PRC, as well as Edwin Montague, a Liberal, because the Liberals were the ruling party.

Henry Massingham, editor of the Liberal magazine *The Nation* wrote of Asquith at this time in November 1914:

'If you want a tonic... look at the Prime Minister. Unquestionably, Mr Asquith is carrying his burden with great courage; with a steady, massive, self reliant, and unswerving confidence which is in itself a moral asset of no slight value.'[21]

The much depleted British Army received a needed boost on 25 September with the arrival of 12,000 Indians in a flotilla at Marseilles; the first Empire troops were arriving. The situation was further helped by Britain's oldest ally, Portugal, offering to supply arms, ammunition and men. They were badly needed for the army was now short of men, having sustained large casualties since the beginning of the war, and on a scale not envisaged in planning beforehand; Britain was not armed, equipped, or counting on playing a large part in a Continental war. The first Battle of Ypres had been the end of the original British Expeditionary Force which had strained every muscle to stop the German offensive in the salient there. The 2nd Highland Light Infantry were typical in that they started the war with 1,000 men, and three months later there were 30 Officers and men left serving.[22] The shortage of available men was acute, though hundreds of thousands were undergoing training.

On 12 November during a debate in the Commons, Mr Walter Long, MP for the Strand constituency in London, rose to make a scathing attack upon the War Office on the matter of allowances for soldiers' wives and families.[23] He thought, not unreasonably, that the War Office organization

34

responsible for paying allowances across Britain was not working very well and that the whole thing should be overhauled to help people who were not getting their money and were going in want. Mr Long's view was very enlightened; he pointed out that in rural areas, many husbands and wives were not actually 'married' in a legal sense of having gone through a ceremony, but were not less 'married' than those who had. Without the marriage certificate women who were actually 'wives' were not getting their husband's separation allowances, and they and their children were going in want. Mr Long, as a rural landowner with huge estates in Wiltshire, was very well qualified to speak on this and he did so to good effect. He thought this matter was holding back recruiting because would be soldiers wished to know their families were taken care of. Although Mr Harold Baker, Financial Secretary to the War Office, made a good reply, Asquith had to agree to a day when this matter could be discussed, and he evidently did not like having to do so, as he referred to Long's speech as a 'prolix and rather vicious attack' in a letter to Venetia.[24]

Walter Long was not a man who could be ignored, especially when he had a good point. He had been one of the two contenders to be the leader of the Conservative Party in 1911, the other being Austen Chamberlain. Since he commanded the support of about 100 MPs, as did Chamberlain, it looked as if a leadership struggle would tear the party apart. Both men had stepped aside for a neutral candidate with no following and no ministerial experience, Andrew Bonar Law. Long was the undisputed leader of the Tory right, known as 'The Squire' a man of great ministerial experience, a man of huge energy and with a reputation for getting things done. Sometimes hot-headed, sometimes ill-advised, once he took a matter up he did not let it go and had very definite opinions which he would relate to all and sundry; sometimes he held contradicting opinions at the same time. He had no great opinion of Asquith, nor Asquith of him; the Premier used the word 'vicious' about him more than once. Now he was taking an interest in recruiting. However he had a particular reason for his attack on the War Office about allowances; he had access to information because he was serving on the National Relief Fund Committee. This had been set up on 6 August by Herbert Samuel, President of the Local Government Board, which post Long had held in the Conservative administration of Balfour. The cross party committee advised the relief organization which was run as a kind of official Charity with the Prince of Wales as its treasurer. Despite the rift between the parties, Mr Long had continued to serve on it, for he had a great sense of duty, even if it meant working with the opposition in pursuit of common goals. Also numbered in the Committee were John Burns, no longer a Cabinet minister, and Ramsay MacDonald of Labour.

This is a paradigm of the Conservative's dilemma; as it was Labour's too. They wished to help. The country was engaged in the biggest war it had ever been in. The national effort was supreme, and they were not in it. They desperately wished to play their part as patriots, as their contribution to the victory while their sons fought, and to do what they saw as the right. As the year wore on this impasse stayed in place.

Lord Crewe, Liberal leader in the Lords, wrote to Lord Hardinge speaking of a 'dangerous energy' building up in the Conservatives at this time.[25] They were playing very little part in the running of the war, had no input to policy and their leader wished to continue the policy of Patriotic non-cooperation indefinitely.

It was in November 1914 that attacks began on Lord Haldane as being too pro-German, castigating him for being far too fond of German language, culture and institutions. Although Conservative newspapers had praised him at the opening of the war because his army reforms had given Britain such an efficient regular army with which to go to war, those same papers now joined in attacks on him, and they went on for months and into 1915. As Stephen Koss showed in 1969 [26] Bonar Law, Edward Carson and Walter Long were well aware of the attacks and wished them to continue. Koss again in 1976 drew attention to their complicity in the deliberate denigration of Haldane:

'Arnold White, who spewed forth his venom in the columns of the Daily Express sent word to Maxse (Editor of the National Review) on 4 February 1915 that he had 'talked at length with Bonar Law, Carson and Long' who indicated 'no desire to abandon the campaign against Haldane just as the scent is burning', but were '...in one way or another... anxious to be present on Whitehall or St James Street when the plump body of the member for Germany swings in the wind between two lamp-posts..[27]

Haldane was one of Asquith's closest and oldest colleagues but he failed to defend him against these attacks in the Press, and the cumulative result over several months was that Haldane became a focus for popular hatred, and a symbol of all that was wrong with the government. The reason was his disdain for them.

Asquith also did not consider that he had to take any notice of what the Press said – they had no mandate to speak – his government had the mandate. Margot Asquith famously said that 'Henry takes no more notice of the Press than St Paul's Cathedral does of gnats', but he was wrong to do so. He was not aware of the power of the Press in this war and saw no reason to act. Yet in this sort of politics, in wartime, perception was all.

On 26 November Margot Asquith wrote in her diary:

'... We have got a million men and they recruit 30,000 a week. Any form of compulsion would stop the whole fine spirit and set all wise men by the ears. From a political point of view, if the Tories go in for conscription, it would be a great lift for us.'[28]

She was not quite correct. The Conservatives did indeed go for conscription, but that issue was the rock upon which the impasse eventually broke, though the route to that end was convoluted and tortuous.

With the SS Themis, the issues were somewhat clearer.

Chapter 3

Iron for Germany

The iron ore unloaded by the Themis could not stay on the quayside. Van Udens were sure of that - Rotterdam was a busy port and whilst the ore sat, it had to be paid for, and took up space that other cargoes could take up, both incoming and outgoing. Quays are not permanent storage facilities. On 11 August Jacks & Co in Glasgow wired Van Udens that they agreed to the discharge of the Themis's ore into lighters; the large barges used on the River Rhine. Most of the ore was on the quayside. Some was still in the hold.[29] They did not know it but matters had moved beyond their control.

On 13 August Jacks & Co sent a letter to Van Udens in Rotterdam expressing their concern that 4,500 tons of iron ore had been delivered to the Phoenix Iron Company - in Germany. Mr Carl Peters was acting as the agent of Jacks & Co in their Duisberg office. He was a reservist officer in the German army; he was apparently rather anxious that the ore be delivered before he was called to join the colours. He had been in communication with Van Udens, in neutral Holland, and they, being neutrals, saw no commercial reason why they should not ship the ore up the River Rhine - so it was done. The delivery of itself did not seem to bother the Jacks directors overly, but they were concerned that they had had no indication that payment would be made; they were also owed money from previous shipments which had not yet been paid. They told Van Udens that they had no authority to deliver the ore, that they could not get in touch with Carl Peters, the Duisburg forwarding agent as it was wartime, and he, as a reservist, had been called up into the German army. The Dutch already knew this of course, but they were in touch with Peters and he wanted the ore delivered in the usual way, which is what Van Udens did.[30]

The next day Jacks wrote again to Van Udens; this letter was damning. Van Udens wished to deliver a further 2,500 tons of ore to Phoenix Iron Company. The British company stated that they had no objection whatever to delivering ore to these 'friends' provided it was possible to get payment for it. They did not wish another ton to go to Germany unless they could get cash for it. They wished Van Udens to arrange for payment to go to their own bankers in Amsterdam before the Germans got another ton. At no point now did they suggest shipping the ore out of the Netherlands to Britain or elsewhere other than Germany.

A further exchange on 18 August indicated that the Germans were quite happy to pay Van Udens the money for what had been delivered, and would pay for the rest as per contract. They would also settle the amounts outstanding for deliveries which had been made before the start of the war. Jacks stated that they would be 'quite willing' upon payment for the Germans to have the Themis's cargo. The letter went on to add that if there was not an absolute prohibition on their doing so, they should be only too glad to send other cargoes to Rotterdam of ore for Germany, and could only hope that things moved in the direction of peace.[31]

Business is business. Payments began to Van Udens on 27 September and amounts were passed to Jacks & Co as follows:

From Krupps of Essen 4 September	£1,161
From Phoenix Ironworks 13 September	£2,719, 4/7d
From Rheinische Stahlwerke 13 September	£5,591, 17/8d
From Krupps of Essen 13 September	£5,853
Ditto 15 September	£2,193
Total	£17,518, 2/3d

That was a handsome amount considering this is what Van Udens passed to Jacks, having already taken their commission. The shareholders and anyone who had money deposited at interest in the firm of Jacks & Co could look forward to no diminution or loss from their dividend from this debacle. Their interests had been protected; unless they were serving at the front of course, or had friends or family facing shells, bullets, guns, etc, that might well, in the very near future, be made of British sourced iron ore. What was done, was done. It might have been unfortunate that the ore had reached the enemy, but at least Jacks had recovered the money; that was something. Looking on the bright side, the enemy had less capital at his disposal now to buy other things. So it could even be seen as a patriotic duty to get the money so as to reduce their funds. Of course, the Directors of Jacks & Co were aware of the Proclamation against trading with the enemy and with the Trading of the Enemy Act; as responsible and intelligent businessmen of good standing, involved in large amounts of international trade, how could they not be?

But at least the matter was ended satisfactorily.

Or so it appeared.[32]

Conservative Differences

Bonar Law was against conscription. As Roy Douglas pointed out, Bonar Law had made a speech in Belfast on 28 September 1914 and considered the question of Compulsion:

'...where the Unionist leader had said that it was not right to put pressure on any man'.[33]

Certainly he had not moved significantly on this issue by 14 December 1914 when he informed the Unionist Agents' Conference that:

'...voluntaryism '...has not failed here. We have got so far, and I am sure we shall get, all the men we need.'[34]

Bonar Law was not alone in his reluctance to consider Conscription, for the Conservative and Unionist Party was not united on the question; some of them had a perfectly valid and ideological and Conservative objection to the whole idea, which was perfectly expressed by Lord Robert Cecil of Chelwood in some speech notes dated 1914 quite late in the year;

'Militarism means the training of a nation to regard war as the chief patriotic duty of every citizen before which all else must give way - to be before else a fighting machine. For this, Conscription, suppression of political liberty, subjection of women, perpetually dwelling on military matters, encouragement of brutality (dueling, bullying, coarseness)... No more preparations should be made than strict requirement of self-defence. Military service therefore should be strictly limited to that. Everyone should indeed be ready to give his life for his country, still more for his religion... to talk therefore of military service as in itself incumbent on all patriots, absurd unless necessary for defence.

Is conscription normally necessary? I think not. Might be essential now if voluntary efforts fail, though I should deeply regret it because voluntary service essential to highest courage. But only acceptable even so as emergency measure. So long as fleet unbeaten this shows Conscription unnecessary. Though in some respect preparation very defective, we have so far done all right.

Finally, to adopt Conscription is to abandon one of our great claims to a higher political ideal than Germany. Curious how passionately anxious Junkers have always been that we should adopt Conscription. Why? Because if not sooner or later their people will want to know why they

40

can't get on without it as well as us. And when that question is asked, English ideals will have won. [35]

These are interesting sentiments from someone whom Asquith regarded as a 'ruffian' who made 'foul attacks' in Parliament. His highly influential brother Hugh Cecil wrote to Bonar Law:

'My Dear Bonar Law; I venture to write to express the hope that nothing may be said to commit the party to any policy of 'national service' or the like in time of peace. Compulsion may be necessary for the war as it was a hundred years ago - tho' I hope not.... And the doctrine that we are to submit to the burden of universal military service for a hundred years in order at the end to finish a great war in one year rather than two seems to me positively silly.

However, I don't want to argue the point; only I am apprehensive that something might be hastily done under the pressure of the war which in calmer times might ruin the party... [36]

Long went on the offensive with a letter to Bonar Law himself on 25 November on the subject of conscription:

'...The procrastination of the government is disastrous, and personally I regret more than I can say that AJB's patriotism and devotion to duty have compelled him to join their counsels because in this as in everything else their craven spirit will lead them to make free use of his name as a buffer between them and any attack. The cry from the front is still for more men... I gather that we now have plenty of rifles and ammunition.... I wish you could see your way to press the government on this point, as their inaction is causing great anxiety in the country and is really dangerous and I think that a private hint from you that we were all profoundly dissatisfied and that there is urgent need something should be done would have a good effect.' [37]

Walter Long was becoming very exercised indeed in a letter to HA Gwynne, about the need for compulsion:

'The Gov ought to go in for Conscription based on population and numbers already join to Colours; they are drawing the lifeblood of our agricultural districts & leaving the streets of some of our towns full as ever of stalwart loafers...' [38]

HA Gwynne was the editor of the right wing Conservative *Morning Post*. Long was not just writing to a friend here, but clearly wished to produce an effect, and that effect was not in accord with the wishes of his party leader and a strain of thought in his own party. One does not write to newspaper editors in such a strain unless one has an object in mind.

Bonar Law himself was also wavering; on the face of it he had ceased co-operation with the government, but on 9 November received a letter from John Boraston, Secretary of the Parliamentary Recruiting Committee[39] asking him to sign a joint letter with Asquith and Henderson on the subject of recruiting, which was to be released to the newspapers; he could hardly refuse.

Walter Long however was not as implacable at this point as he might have appeared – indeed he might be labeled at somewhat opportunist, this being the same man who was to declare in the Commons on 8 February 1915:

'I am a firm believer—and who is not in this country—in the voluntary system...'[40]

He was perhaps, at this point, still feeling his way and unsure of his support.

With one potential rival in the War Council, another consulting with Lloyd George at the Treasury, and another attempting to divert party policy down paths he did not wish to follow, his policy of inactivity was making his position shaky if any large dissatisfaction with his leadership arose. To make matters worse, in the War Council on 16 December, Balfour put forward the argument that indiscriminate recruiting could have a very bad effect on the economy of the nation. Asquith agreed straightaway and described it in his letter to the King as:

'...a most important question...Mr Balfour undertook to write a paper on the subject'.[41]

Not only was a leading Conservative ex-Prime Minister now shaping policy, but whatever Bonar Law's reaction to Long's pressure might have been, even if he had wanted to change policy, he would set himself up against Balfour. As to Asquith - by his agreement with Balfour, he had signaled that his mind was open to an organized system of recruiting of some kind.

The prominent Liberal Unionist Peer Lord Selborne was reported in the *Aberdeen Daily Journal* on 3 December praising Lord Kitchener for bringing a new and more powerful army into existence between midsummer and Christmas. Yet on 10 December he had a letter in *The Times* pointing out that this might not be enough and that the government would probably have to have some sort of compulsion eventually. It would be criminal folly to pull men away from important work, so some sort of system should be devised now in case it were needed. Clearly the matter crossed party boundaries and there was ground for common endeavour. Selborne had started out as a Liberal, but became a Liberal Unionist, serving in the Conservative government of Lord Salisbury. He is a good example of how the issue of compulsion tore a line across the party boundaries.

Geoffrey Dawson, Editor of *The Times*, had a talk with Bonar Law on 29 December 1914 and made a note of his talk. He suggested to Bonar Law that the real weakness in the country was that the government had failed to employ anyone but members of their own party for really responsible work. No doubt that Chamberlain, Long, Balfour and others had been invited to serve on various committees but this really did not make full use of them. He called attention to Selborne's letter on compulsory service, wondered if anyone was entrusted with looking at it, and spoke of lack of coordination and supreme control:

'He was inclined to agree with all this, but I found him very much opposed at the present stage to anything like a Coalition government. He said that he himself would feel very uncomfortable in it...' [42]

By October 1914, less than 3 months after the beginning of the war, Parliament, at Kitchener's behest, sanctioned the creation of a 5th new army. Since 5 August Kitchener had laid the foundations for no less than 30 new divisions; it was an achievement unprecedented in British history.[43] For most of the recruits flooding in there were no weapons, uniforms, living accommodation, cookhouses, medical centres, rifle ranges, artillery ranges, basic equipment of any sort. To speak of compulsory service to get men at this date must have seemed to many people to be absurd.

Dutch Letters

At the beginning of November 1914 Mr Montague Rousseau Emanuel, an assistant censor at the War Office in London, was handed two letters to read which had just arrived from Holland, from a company called Van Udens. At this stage of the war not all letters were being read, but a Post Office Censor had sent them to Emanuel because they caused him some concern. Having read the letters Emanuel agreed that they needed looking into and sent them to the Home Office. In turn the Home Office sent them to the office of Mr Hart, the Procurator Fiscal in Glasgow. Mr Hart in turn was directed by Thomas McKinnon-Wood, Secretary for Scotland, to make out a warrant to search the premises of Jacks & Co. He was to investigate and examine the correspondence and associated papers in the offices of Jacks & Co, also of Glasgow. With Mr Hart was Robert MacFarlane, chartered accountant of Glasgow who stated later in court that he had been:

'commissioned by the Secretary of State for Scotland to examine all the productions in the case, including the correspondence and the financial arrangement existing between Messrs Jacks and Van Uden, and other firms in Germany.' [44]

It was more usual for the Chartered Accountant investigating a company to do so at the behest of the Procurator, but evidently the Secretary of State was taking a close interest in the case. McKinnon Wood, MP for Glasgow St Rollox, was a close and trusted friend and colleague of Mr Asquith. In fact he was closer than most, as both he and Asquith represented Scottish constituencies, and the Secretary for Scotland, in the smaller pond of Scottish politics, had to work closely with the President of the Scottish Liberal Association, who was Asquith. Wood was a man who, like Asquith, did not say much in Cabinet, but was regarded as a solid and competent politician and administrator who had done his job well since 1912, and who would continue in office as long as Asquith did. He was a safe pair of hands. Any significance attached to his personally setting off the search warrant and investigation for Jacks & Co the family firm of the Conservative leader, has however to be conjecture.

Mr Hart and a body of police then went to the offices of Jacks & Co and served their warrant, seizing all paperwork they wished, taking it away for examination. The directors of the company gave fullest cooperation with the Procurator Fiscal and it did not take long to establish that Jacks & Co appeared to have traded with the enemy.

Four of the directors were questioned. Two of them, Robert Hetherington and Henry Wilson, were arrested and charged with trading with the enemy. They were released on heavy bail - set at £2,000 each - a considerable sum in 1914. The other two directors faced investigation. At this stage none of the men' names appeared in the press - for some of them that was to come later.

The transaction with the Germans arose out of a contract signed before the war and the delivery of the ore had not been made by Jacks & Co but by their Dutch agents. Furthermore, the proclamation against trading with the enemy had been made after the Royal Navy had allowed the Themis to proceed on her way to Holland. More importantly, the Act against the same, had been passed on 8 August 1914, the day after the Themis had docked in Rotterdam. It appeared that the directors had nothing to worry about. However, in a curious political twist, the House of Commons amended the Trading with the Enemy Act on 25 November:

(1) 'Section one of the principal Act shall apply to a person who during the present War attempts, or directly or indirectly offers, or proposes or agrees, or has since the fourth day of August, nineteen hundred and fourteen, attempted or directly or indirectly offered or proposed or agreed, to trade with the enemy within the meaning of that Act in like manner as it applies to a person who so trades or has so traded. (Trading with the Enemy Act Amendment Act) [45]

So now the act was to apply retrospectively - and the directors of Jacks & Co faced disgrace, heavy fines, and imprisonment.

All this might seem to a lay observer to be rather a legal anomaly. An unfortunate and draconian injustice in the making. A product of the stress of the times and the workings of the war. Certainly the notion of making the Trading with the Enemy Act retrospective was rather a blow for the directors of Jacks, for although what they had done with the ore was legally and morally questionable before the amendment, it was unquestionably illegal after the amendment.

They personally were in deep trouble, their company name would suffer - and it had a very high reputation indeed in the Glasgow Steel Ring, a most prestigious trading association, and their shares and business could suffer greatly if they had been trading with the enemy. They were highly regarded and released regular bulletins on the state of the world iron and steel market, where they were taken very seriously indeed. Of course anyone associated with such a company, if it was found guilty, would be utterly disgraced.

Jacks & Co was the family firm of Andrew Bonar Law, where he had worked for years, founding his fortune before entering politics. Members of his family were prominent amongst its executives and officials and his much loved brother Jack, to whom he was very close, was a director. Further, Bonar Law was in the habit of using the firm as his bank and had £6,525 deposited at interest in the company at this very moment. The two directors who had been arrested were close personal friends of Bonar Law of many years standing. To think that he was not upset and emotionally disturbed by their arrest would attribute to him a detachment which he certainly did not possess.

This company had just made a profit from dealing iron ore to the Germans. A substance used to make bullets, shells and guns with which to kill British soldiers; and the newspapers were full of battles and death, along with much anti-German hysteria. Prince Louis of Battenberg, the First Sea Lord was receiving abuse merely for having a German name and was soon to be replaced after being forced into resignation because of his German birth and parentage. Atrocity stories about what the Germans had done in Belgium, of murdered priests and babies on bayonets, were common currency.

Prime Minister Asquith, writing to Venetia on 18 December told her of a conversation he had with Pamela McKenna:

' Pamela declares that Bonar Law's brother and Partner in Glasgow has been caught 'trading with the enemy' and is now only allowed out on bail for £5,000 - an amusing development. [46]

So not only did the Prime Minister know of it, although the version was somewhat inaccurate, but the wife of the Home Secretary, a known society gossip, and presumably a whole swathe of the ruling class because of that. Here were the germs of a political scandal, strong enough to blow a storm which could sweep political careers away into oblivion, amusing or not. Common knowledge in the Westminster Village, it did not appear in the newspapers, or at least not in any form that could harm Bonar Law. The peacetime freedom of the Press was not in normal operation. And Asquith found it 'amusing,' as well he might, considering Conservative conduct over the Marconi Scandal the year before. Lloyd George and Rufus Isaacs had been pilloried in both Parliament and the press for their alleged insider dealings in shares in the Marconi company. The Conservatives had taken great delight in pillorying them and calling for their heads; Asquith had saved them by asserting in Parliament his complete confidence in them, but the furore had been loud and acrimonious. Any hint that Bonar Law was involved in a firm which had traded with the enemy could unleash a storm about his head which many Liberals would have relished. Revenge in Politics may be best served cold, and on this occasion presented itself freely on a plate of iron made in Germany.

No such storm happened. Ever.

Not at this time or in the months leading up to the trial, was the matter referred to in Parliament. And in the Press it was censored in some places, no names being mentioned where they could have been. All it would have taken would have been one question in the House to have deeply embarrassed Bonar Law and put him onto the defensive at a time when he and his confederates were attacking Lord Haldane as 'the member for Germany'. The Liberals stayed quiet.

Why?

Bonar Law in Trouble

Bonar Law's life was not an easy one as the New Year began. His policy of Patriotic Opposition was causing some of his front bench members to chafe at the bit. Walter Long wrote on 1 January to a friend of his, but a friend with a certain amount of clout. Colonel Charles A'Court Repington was the War Correspondent of the Times and was a personal friend of the Commander of the British Expeditionary Force (BEF), Sir John French. At a time when no war correspondents were able to go to the front because it simply was not allowed, Repington was able to go and visit French at his Headquarters and they would talk freely. Long had thus a direct line into the ear of Sir John:

' *At present I can see no evidence that we are not living from hand to mouth, taking steps without realizing their inevitable consequences and liabilities tomorrow and the day after..... we want the number (of recruits) stated. Then how are we to get them. The voluntary system has worked splendidly but it is beginning to tell severely on the agricultural districts especially in dairy districts.... I am therefore for compulsion based upon population and numbers already gone to the colours... town loafers who will never come unless they are compelled. They will make good soldiers and will not be missed as they contribute a minimum.*

Reply from Repington:
'I am quite clear that we ought to organize compulsion at once so that we may be able to apply it at any moment. It takes a long time to arrange, as you know well, but Lord K knows nothing of this side of his business. I think you will have to give Tennant a good heckling on the subject.' [47]

Walter Long needed no encouragement from Repington in order to air the question of compulsion, though he must have known his party leader's views on the matter and that within his own party many did not like the notion. There was a strong strain of Conservative belief that thought that it was anti-Conservative to force the individual into uniform at the service of the state and by doing so Britain would stoop to exactly the sort of Germanic militarism that she was fighting against. Bonar Law was among these. When Long pursued this idea and wrote to Bonar Law on 4 January, it was not about general compulsion that he spoke of:

'...I had a long talk with Lansdowne and Curzon today and I think they are of opinion that there must be some criticism and demands for fuller information on Army and Navy questions. I am confident it is necessary in the interests of the country and that it can be administered without any controversy of a party character or without any appearance of a division of opinion in the country...I feel we ought to have a considered policy and well thought out plans... I am strongly of opinion that we ought to make Compulsory Cadet military training a part of our party programme. Curzon I know shares this view and I did not understand Lansdowne to dissent from it. There are other matters on which I think we ought to make our mind (sic) and give a lead to the country but these we must of course discuss... I feel very strongly that a heavy responsibility rests upon the opposition and that we ought to make our position clear at a time of such great National importance. [48]

This was not rebellion, but in calling for more criticism he was attempting to change party policy from patriotic opposition, to active opposition, a suggestion, but not a welcome one. The reference to compulsory Cadet Training in schools was one for which a section of the Conservative Party had been campaigning for some years before the war. Long was evidently not content with sitting on the sidelines. Nor was he the only Conservative grandee so disgruntled.

On 6 January 1915 Lord Curzon, evidently frustrated by lack of information about the war stood in the Lords and made a speech in the newly reconvened house, which included:

'We have been at War for five months. I am not going, to say, although I think I know, the numbers of men that we have at the Front. That would be an unwise and unpatriotic thing to do. I go further and say that I think the numbers which the Secretary of State for War has sent to the Front are amazing; and on August 3 last, when war commenced, if we had been told that in five months he was going to put this number at the Front, there is hardly one of us who would have believed it possible. I say that to the credit of the War Office.' [49]

Nonetheless, although he recognized the scale of this amazing achievement which had taken place in 5 months, he was disappointed at a 'sonic' level because recruiting according to Kitchener, was proceeding normally and he had wished to hear that it was proceeding 'abnormally'. There followed some further criticism about what arrangements were in place to ensure the future supply of men, but this was all rather unreasonable. Asquith told Venetia on 7 January that by June Britain would have a million men either at the front or available, 400,000 special reserve for overseas service and a Home Defence army of 500,000 which for 5 months of war, was astonishing. The fact is that Curzon did not have the detailed information he wished to have and only the vaguest notion based on unofficial sources about recruiting figures. He complained that if he and his friends asked questions they were treated like naughty children.

Kitchener later told Margot Asquith that he could have shot Curzon with his own hand for his lack of praise for all the splendid fellows going into the Army and his attempted flattery; and that he had walked out, along with Lord Derby. Kitchener's irritation is understandable, though the animosity between him and Lord Curzon had long roots; at that time there was no shortage of men - in fact quite the reverse, for the War Department was straining every nerve to equip and accommodate them.

Two days later Earl Midleton a very influential Conservative and Unionist, raised the matter of the organization of recruiting, in the Lords and Lord Selborne then opined:

'It must be in the minds of all of us that if our voluntary system does not produce all the men that are required for the completion of this tremendous task, and produce them soon enough, we may have to fall back upon that

inherent obligation which lies on every citizen to defend the hearths and homes and the liberties of his country. The United States of America had to do that in the Civil War. They had to enforce that inherent obligation in order to complete that war, and we may have to do the same. What I want to point out to the Government is this, that if the moment should come when the nation was convinced that to perform the task it had taken in hand it must call on all its able-bodied citizens to fulfill this inherent obligation'[50]

Evidently the long break had given rise to the Tory grandees discussing the matter of manpower and recruiting; they were also concerned that the wrong men were being recruited as many vital workers had to be sent back to their jobs because they were more useful doing that than fighting the enemy. In this they were completely correct - the recruiting of men had gone on in such an disorganized and uncoordinated way that industry was beginning to feel its effects badly. Also, in talking to officers at the front during the winter of 1914-15 they related constantly that there was a shortage of men, which there was. Anthony Farrar Hockley outlined in *'Death of an Army'* in 1967 how the Regular Army BEF had been decimated at the First battle of Ypres where they had stopped a force seven times their own strength; Sir John French, Commander in Chief of the BEF was wanting every man he could get, but he meant that he wanted soldiers and those men who had joined up at the outbreak of the war were still in training. If the compulsionists were looking for an issue on which they might disagree with the Liberals, namely that of compulsory service, they must have been rather surprised by Lord Haldane who stood up and in a long speech declared:

'But I wish to add this—I have said it before, in Parliament and out of Parliament—that by the Common Law of this country it is the duty of every subject of the realm to assist the Sovereign in repelling the invasion of its shores and in defence of the realm. That is a duty which rests on no Statute but is inherent in the Constitution of the country. It has been laid down— noble Lords can look up the authority for themselves—that any subject at a time of emergency may be asked to give himself and his property for the defence of the nation. Therefore compulsory service is not foreign to the Constitution of this country. Given a great national emergency I think it is your duty to resort to it. I can conceive a state of things in which we might resort to it. Therefore I do not want to take up any attitude based on abstract principle about this. In time of peace I have always told your Lordship; that I thought that to resort to compulsory service would be a

bad thing; and at this time even I do not think it would be a good thing. Unless it becomes a final necessity, which it has not as yet, it should not be resorted to. We hope to solve our problem by this magnificent response which is being made, and which gives us, after all, men who are to a certain extent picked, who come because of their enthusiasm, and men who are better than the dead level which compulsory service gives you. Therefore it is with reluctance that we should go to that. But at a time of national necessity every other consideration must yield to national interest, and we should bar nothing in the way of principle if it should become necessary.' [51]

A statement like this from Haldane, Lord Chancellor, architect of the new BEF and the Territorial Army, Liberal ideologue and close friend of Asquith made it crystal clear to all that no consideration of ideology would prevent them from doing what was necessary, should it prove so. Compulsion was not an issue which need divide the parties, was not a bone of contention and no need for a quarrel.

But of course Kitchener had performed a major miracle in that thousands of men had volunteered for the forces and were undergoing training at that very moment. There was absolutely no need in January 1915 to compel men into the Army. Kitchener was justifiably indignant about calls on him to support compulsion as he told Asquith on 12 January because although he had lost 80,000 men after 5 months of war, he nevertheless had 1.75 million men in training. [52]

The only excuse that the government can have in not organizing the recruiting of the new armies better was that they had not expected the war to be long. Kitchener did, but it was not his responsibility to ensure a balance in recruitment, just to build his armies. The Conservative criticism on the subject of lack of organization is thus justified and justifiable, though on the subject of numbers, was merely inaccurate. Kitchener had done what he said he would do with great success, and would continue to do so. Nonetheless, as he told Venetia, Asquith smiled at the thought of Curzon and Midleton, who had taken the country into the Boer war with no preparation at all and now did nothing but *'cavil & carp & criticize'*. He had a point.

Selborne however, had moved the matter a little further and brought up the subject of organizing the nation's resources by setting up systems to supply the army with men, and yet retain those needed to supply the war at home - metal workers, engineers, chemists and so on. This was an entirely different and far more contentious issue, especially for Labour, who would see that as regimentation of Labour - an attempt to chain the masses. Syndicalists and socialists had long suspected that this was the ultimate goal of capitalists, and Hilaire Belloc's book *The Servile State*, which pictured this happening, had been published in 1912, and was a popular read among Fabians and Socialists. The number of men flocking into the army was beginning to affect production in industries, as a Command Report would show the government very shortly.

On 12 January the shortage of food due to the shortage of dock labour was discussed in Cabinet, and Kitchener suggested that women could be used to make up the shortage of labour. When it was pointed out that women were not used to such work he retorted that they were being used in Zanzibar. Evidently this made an impression on Asquith because he asked Venetia to suggest trades where women could take the place of men, himself suggesting clerks, shop men and bus and tram conductors. Supply of labour was becoming an issue in the nation.[53]

The frustration of the Conservatives was well reflected in a letter from Bonar Law to *The Times* on 9 January where he reminded people that the suspension of free Parliamentary attack had been made in the reflection that the Opposition might console themselves that they would have preliminary knowledge on subjects of importance and that their opinions would be heard. This had been made in response to a letter from Lord Crewe to *The Times* the previous day which seemed to imply that the opposition shared in some responsibility with government. Bonar Law acknowledged the fact that he received despatches from Sir John French but stated that neither he nor Lord Lansdowne, Conservative leader in the Lords received any information about the conduct of the war which had not been published first. Clearly he was no more happy with the situation than Curzon. Next day:

'Crewe's letter is extraordinary and I am afraid I must add disingenuous...I have been unable to trace Austen's letter to which he refers in his. I ventured to suggest (via Dawkins over the telephone) that it might be worthwhile to admit that HMG had shown us civility in the matter of communicating telegrams, and that there had been useful co-operation in regard to certain subjects, although in regard to steps taken or contemplated for the presentation of the war we have not been consulted at all....'[54]

He obviously wished to avoid any suggestion that the opposition shared in or were responsible in anyway for what the government did, and was anxious to point it out. On 10 January Lord Hugh Cecil wrote a memorandum to his own brother, Lord Robert, a very confidential communication. He argued that there was much to be said in favour of cooperation of moderate men on both sides, but such an alliance might not be created until after the war was over. A great advantage would be that Conservative leaders like Bonar Law and Chamberlain would be severed from the type of Tory who read *The Morning Post* and *The National Review* and an effectual party would be created. However, he saw Lloyd George as a future enemy of that government.[55] He believed that Asquith, Grey and Haldane would be glad to have opportunities of working with the Conservative leaders, though he did not think Churchill would be easy to work with, and he found the idea of working with Asquith 'repugnant'.

'It is obvious that a section of the Cabinet are every pleased at the opportunity of working with leaders of the Opposition; and coupled with other indications I think it may be regarded as pretty certain that they would be glad to take part in some kind of Coalition, if circumstances make such a course feasible. In this section of the Cabinet must certainly be reckoned Grey, Asquith, Churchill and Haldane and possibly others. It is important we should consider what attitude we should adopt, supposing some such modification of the political situation took place.' [56]

Cecil thought that the Conservatives should take advantage of the 'no party politics' atmosphere to build a 'golden bridge' over which willing Liberals could cross and cooperate with Conservatives. To that end he thought they should make it easy for the moderate Liberals and refrain from attacking them; quite obviously he was quite prepared to consider coalition of it were offered. In essence he was proposing what Asquith was already doing, and what some willing Conservatives were already doing.

Bonar Law though was at pains to point out in the House and in the newspapers that though the government was receiving some assistance from Conservatives, there was no partnership between the parties and the Conservatives had no responsibility for war policy. Crewe wrote to him in placatory fashion:

'I see today that you express surprise at a statement of mine on Saturday last regarding the information upon public affairs possessed by the Opposition. I don't want to continue a newspaper discussion but I venture

to ask you whether our difference does not arise - as differences often do - from our using the same phrase to describe two different things... was thinking not only of the valuable help given in matters of finance ; but of your own services on the Board of Trade Committee, of Long's on Relief of Distress and of Fellowes on Agriculture, to say nothing of such men as Robert Cecil ... And on the particular question of the conduct and prosecution of the war I think it is fair to point out that only half-a-dozen of us Liberal ministers enjoy the same means of studying the present and future aspects of the subject as Balfour does from joining us on the small sub committee which considers these matters with the principle experts, where his cooperation is of course enormously valuable. I need not say that whatever the pros and cons may be of conducting such a war as this by coalition methods, I never hinted that the former were all secured by such a measure of cooperation as we have tried to effect; my original remark in the House to which Austen Chamberlain took exception, was only made because thought Curzon had ignored this side of the matter altogether.' [57]

It is fair comment to point out that several Conservatives, including Bonar Law himself, had actually been taking part in government business. It is interesting particularly to see Crewe point out that Balfour, by virtue of being in the War Council, had access to information not enjoyed by all the Liberal Ministers. Balfour evidently felt at this time that his party leader might find his position of cooperating with the government a rather odd one, and wrote to Lansdowne offering to withdraw his services from the government. He would do so but was averse to the idea, he was too old to fight and felt that this was all he could do for the general cause. Lansdowne also later discussed it with Law, but astonishingly Law was inclined to take Balfour's 'advice on the whole position',[58] so Balfour continued his one man coalition arrangement with Bonar Law's blessing. Whatever Bonar Law's scruples about the matter, there is little doubt that coalition was in the air. Asquith, and other Liberals had been, with some consistency, seeking the participation of certain Conservatives in the business of government and whatever else may be said in public, or officially, certain Conservatives had been lending their assistance to the government. In truth the idea of coalition was such an obvious one that it would probably have been stranger if the government did not seek to move towards it, than if it did. There was an obvious reticence on the part of many people in both parties, but not, apparently, on the Liberal front bench, or in one section of the Conservative party.

Chapter 4

The Agitation of Mr Long

On 13 January Asquith's War Council met from 12.00 noon until 2.00 pm, then sat again after a break for lunch.[1] At 4.00 pm Asquith was sitting next to Sir John French as the Council was discussing Churchill's plans to force the passage of the Dardanelles and bombard Constantinople. Sir John Fisher was against the idea as he wished to attack Germany through the Baltic. Kitchener was against it because it would take troops that he did not have, but Churchill thought the Navy could do it without soldiers. The Cabinet Secretary, Maurice Hankey, who had studied and written much on the topic of warfare on the littoral, warned that it would need soldiers in order to succeed. This was a critical meeting, during which Asquith was writing a letter to his muse. He maintained, as he wrote afterwards, an almost unbroken silence until the end, when, as was his habit, he summed up in the manner, as Churchill said - of a great judge - and gave his conclusions. This was his usual manner in Cabinet. However, it is quite inexcusable that at a moment like this when concentration was needed, the Prime Minister should be so distracted. He was paying a certain amount of attention though when another, and perhaps even more important issue came under discussion. Afterwards, in his customary letter to the King, Asquith referred to:

'....The congestion in the ports of London and Liverpool through the scarcity of labour, in consequence of recruiting... the Home Office should concert measures to deal with the Labour difficulty.'[2]

This was of course the heart of the real problem with recruiting, which was not that the Army was short of men. Plainly it was not. The problem was that too little organization had been put into which men went into the army. The allocation of manpower needed to be controlled and if it were not then shortage of labour in the docks was merely one sign of what would inevitably follow. Measures to deal with the labour shortage were needed, but if there was an element of compulsion then there would be difficulties. John Burn's sentiments were shared far more powerfully by many in Labour:

'A clear morning - the ground white with snow - soon turned to sleet hail and rain. In this awful downpour I walked to Waterloo from Local GB with some 300 grenadiers strong, cheery handsome fellows whose strength was *delightful to witness, whose buoyant spirits no weather could depress, singing as they strode, exultant in the joy of life, conquering the climate with a radical will. Splendid because simple....I was, with the marching policemen, the only person to see them pass by at the corner of Belvedere Road. These men, marching to their doom profoundly touched me as with a rousing cheer they responded to my salute by taking off my hat, and wishing them good luck, and I am afraid, goodbye. In a reverie, thoughts crowding upon me I almost cried as I saw these magnificent industrials sacrificed as the victims of the dynasties and their diplomats...* [3]

There were many in the Trades Union movement and in the Labour Party who saw the war in terms of a Capitalist plot to chain and ensnare the workers by distracting them from class struggle into nationalistic wars. There were great profits to be gained in such a war and Socialists across Europe regarded the whole struggle with great suspicion. If they came out against the war then they could stop it very quickly with large-scale strikes.

Bonar Law was also turning the problem of manpower and control over in his mind, inevitably given the agitations of some of his party, but he also received some strong advice from the Professor of Constitutional Law at University College, London, AF Pollard.

'Conscription does not have a constitutional basis- a conversion of feudal contract into political obligation, extended to parties never in contract, to enforce by common law right of force which does not exist'. [4]

That was clear enough, and completely in accord with his personal feelings against compulsion. He may also have been having other thoughts as to ending his stance of 'Patriotic Opposition' and opening the gates to more cooperation with the Liberals; the Daily Chronicle had evidently been listening to some rumours which Edward Gould, Conservative MP for Worcester, hoped were true because he simply had to write to Bonar Law and tell him so:

'I do hope what the Chronicle foretells is true that you and Ld Lansdowne are to join the War Committee.' [5]

It is likely that Asquith would not have been averse to such a thing happening given his obvious willingness to have opposition members undertaking government tasks, but as yet it could not happen, for there would be opposition to it in both parties. The Conservative right were against it, as they were about to demonstrate amply. On Saturday 23

January Lloyd George was a guest of the Asquith's at Walmer Castle and told Margot that he thought the opposition were desperate for a coalition, which she agreed with, but thought they were more desperate to get rid of Haldane and McKenna, the two Liberals they despised most. Lloyd George's reply was interesting:

- *'We've got their best man - Arthur Balfour; who else is there?'*[6]

He obviously did not rate the other Conservative leaders very highly, but in thinking they were desperate for a coalition, he was not referring to all of them. The resentment on the Conservative right had been simmering for long enough by the last week of January 1915 and now it began to boil over.

On 24 January 1915 Lord Curzon, who had also contended for the leadership of the Conservative party in 1911, wrote to Walter Long, who was increasingly frustrated in pressing for what he thought essential to win the war - compulsory service. Long was convinced that the army was short of men, and that the only way to get them was to force them into uniform. He was also deeply concerned about the unfairness of a system where some men went off to fight and other 'shirkers' stayed at home and would not do their bit. To this patriotic and vigorous man with his sons and numerous friends in the military it seemed obvious that there had to be conscription. He had believed for a long time in some form of National Service, being involved in the National Service League since well before the outbreak of war. For national efficiency at a time of national crisis there had to be conscription, and at this time he could not see why it should not be brought in straight away; he was to moderate this view in due course. Curzon's letter referred to the Parliamentary Recruiting Committee having been set up:

'under the patronage and with the aid of the organization of both political parties...Now we are not allowed to hear anything about the results...'[7]

Curzon's anger at being excluded from helping with the war effort was obvious, but he aimed it at the Government. The most effective change, that could bring about the best resolution to his discontent however, was in his own leaders' policy, which he knew very well. That same day he circulated a memorandum to his fellow shadow Cabinet members setting out his views and aligning himself with Long.

'I agree with Mr Walter Long in thinking that the relations between the govt and the opposition, if not already intolerable, are quite likely before long to become so. The position appears to be this. We are expected to give a mute, almost unquestioning support to everything done by the govt to maintain a patriotic silence about the various blunders that have been committed in connection with the war (eg Goeben. Audacious), Hogue Cressy Abukir, Antwerp, E Africa, Cradock, Formidable, our submarines, Yrmouth, Hartlepool etc etc to dismantle our party machinery, to forget all party advantage, and allow...measures such as the Plural Voting Bill to be carried\over our heads... in other words the government have all the advantages, while we have all the drawbacks, of a coalition. They tell us nothing or next to nothing of their plans yet they pretend that our leaders share their knowledge and their responsibilities. If we ask perfectly legitimate questions in the H of L we are treated as though we were thought Children, even Lord Lucas. The S of S for war reads his efficacious memoranda of platitudes known to everybody, is acclaimed by the Liberal Press as having delivered a lucent dispensed oration and scored off their ineffectual antagonists' he interpolates a curt affirmative or negative and the solitary speech to which he deigns to listen and he then marches out and leaves the rest of the debate to colleagues who either affect to know nothing or screen their silence behind his authority'[8]

The unmistakable note of exasperation here may be understandable, but it is there by Asquith's design. If the Conservatives were to keep themselves in splendid isolation, then there was a price - lack of information; and that lack of information was bound to breed frustration and discontent, but not only at Asquith, for sooner or later the Conservative leadership would come in for criticism too. Long also sent a memorandum to his senior Conservative colleagues proposing a statement to the press that they supported compulsion, and urging the government to produce 'a return of the population', an idea which later became coalition policy and the genesis of the National Register. [9]

John Stubbs identified this in 1975 as an overt challenge to Bonar Law's political strategy, and implicitly to his authority as leader of his party in the Commons, which it certainly was.[10]

Bonar Law felt exactly the same way as Lord Lansdowne, Conservative leader in the Lords, but they did not feel that they had sufficient information on which to act. This at least was his public stance, but he and Lansdowne stretched the truth very thinly on this matter of consultation. Both he and Bonar Law actually did receive telegrams from the War Office and the Foreign Office to keep them informed as to what was going on.[11] The government might not supply information officially, but individual ministers did. Lord Crewe supplied Curzon with information and Arthur Balfour, at the heart of things, had no problems in communicating whatever he wished to Lansdowne and Law. The shadow Cabinet, unofficially, had the information it needed for discussion of many issues. His caution on this matter may be explained by his feeling uncomfortable about receiving it whilst others did not. Walter Long was a very powerful force to be discontent with him, and Bonar Law did not wish to appear to be too cooperative with the Liberals because Long actually wished to oppose them and Long was a power in the party.

On 27 January Walter Long called a meeting of 27 back-bench Conservatives at 25 Victoria Street (the HQ of the Irish Unionists), to push the ideas of conscription and economic warfare. It had its genesis from an initiative, seemingly by two Conservative back benchers, Ernest Pollock and Basil Peto. Peto was MP for Devizes and a neighbour of Walter Long who had previously been MP for Devizes himself.

Interestingly, one of the members who attended was Stanley Baldwin, hardly the archetype of a rebel. Baldwin initiated a motion to canvass support and campaign for a national organization of manpower, the members of which would send deputations to ministers to lobby for their cause. The membership of this group grew rapidly amongst the right wing backbenchers who regarded Long as their natural leader.[12] The group appears to have decided to set up a Unionist Business Committee to represent the interests of British business in wartime, and to focus economic warfare as a weapon against the Germans. With a caucus of opinion behind him Long felt empowered to make his next move, though he knew full well that his leaders did not wish it:

'I incline to a statement in the Press, signed by the two leaders of the party and if this statement could include a definite declaration that in order to distribute the burden of Military Service equitably they were prepared to support a system of compulsory military service for the period of the war I believe it would give a healthy and much desired lead to the country...[13]

He spoke of 60-70% of troops being married, and of the 'vast empire:

'I have suggested to the War Office that there should be a return of the population of all recruiting areas and the proportion of men serving with

59

the colours, whether recruited before the 5 August or afterwards. This would show what percentage in each area has gone to the colours. Compulsion would then follow according to these figures... I only throw this out as a suggestion.'

Long was not the leader of the party, but he was attempting to set the party's policy and build up support for his view, which was not shared with his leaders. The reaction was swift, Lansdowne replying the next day:

'... whatever we decide to do I would not raise the question of compulsory service at this moment, although here again we cannot be content to let matters rest where they were left by Haldane and Lucas in the House of Lords'. [14]

This was a quite clear statement to Long that the party leaders did not wish at this time to consider compulsion, and that he should drop it. He had been told to behave. It was clear enough to Long, for that is what he did - at least in public, for the moment. Lansdowne wrote another letter to him on the same day:

'My Dear Walter
Your letter of the 27th as to recruiting for the regular army I should like to talk to you about before taking further action. The percentage mentioned in Tennant's note appears to be low but I should like further information as to our alleged shortcomings. I agree that we should not bleed the villages too severely. In some of the towns a considerable proportion of the men of military age are, I suspect, engaged upon industries with which we cannot afford to play tricks while the war is in progress and the vast body of soldiers who are now training within the country must require a great number of people to supply their needs...' [15]

The matter of compulsion exercised Lansdowne's mind somewhat as he wrote to Bonar Law on 28 January, stating his and Curzon's view that compulsory service should not be pushed now, as it would confuse the issue and lay the Conservatives open to hostile criticism. It is important that Lansdowne spoke of the 'alleged' shortcomings also, for Long had no proof that there was or would be a shortage of recruits. The alleged shortage had no figures whatsoever to back it up; if the government was to be challenged then it had to be done not at half cock, but fully researched, and on certain ground. However, Lansdowne also wrote to Bonar Law on that day speaking of:

'defining our position to HMG... we must make up our minds as to the sort of conditions for which we desire to press. Curzon suggests they should include - a. The abandonment of all party legislation. b. The taking of the leaders of the opposition into full confidence about all important matters connected with the conduct of the war etc.... Curzon is, I think, quite right that, whatever be done, we should not bring in at this stage the question of compulsory service. To do so would confuse the issue, to say nothing of laying ourselves open to a considerable body of hostile criticism. A move is likely to be made, probably in our House, in favour of compulsory Cadet training, which I have always strongly supported, but that is another story'[16]

The notion of coalition hovered unspoken and sometimes spoken, in the air, and it appears from Lansdowne's letter that he was not alone in thinking what terms they might ask for as their price for entry into what would, effectively, have to be one. Long wanted to see some sort of national government, but not, as it transpired later, a coalition, which he was vehement against. Curzon seems to have been quite undecided – it is difficult to see how the leaders of the opposition could be taken into fullest confidence about all important matters unless they were prepared to accept also some responsibility for how they were carried out. Information without input would be just as useless as sitting saying nothing – the logical price for negotiating any postponement of a general election keeps coming down to the same inevitable answer, sooner or later, and that answer was coalition.

Lansdowne went on to say that a move for compulsory cadet training would shortly be made in the Lords. The Liberals were well aware of this move and it was potentially embarrassing unless the Liberals backed the move, because the Conservatives commanded a considerable majority in the upper house. Asquith may have had other ideas; if the Tory back benchers wanted cadet training so badly that they were agitating strongly for it against their own leadership, then cadet training had the potential to be the carrot in a Liberal attempt to bring more Conservatives into participation in government. Bonar Law replied to Lansdowne on the 29 January; his reply, copied to Long shows starkly what the Conservative dilemma was:

'I know how unsatisfactory the present position is, for it means that we are conducting the most difficult war in which we have engaged probably in regard to which the nation is united, but half the nation distrusts the men

61

who are carrying it on. That is a very difficult position and might be found impossible; but in my judgment, much as I dislike the present position there are I think only two alternatives open to us; one is to go on as we are doing, without responsibility and with a very limited amount of criticism ... or to face a coalition. The latter proposal I should certainly be against, and on the whole, therefore, I am reluctantly driven to the conclusion that the only proper course for us in the meantime is to continue on the lines on which we have acted since the war began, [17]

Long, as it turned out, did not agree. He wanted an active opposition, but he did not want a coalition and did not see one as an inevitable result of criticizing the Government. There was a disparity of views between himself and the party leaders. As to Bonar Law's statement that he would be against coalition – he could hardly say that he wanted one at this stage because many of his party would resist the idea.

If the possibility of a compulsory national cadet force was a carrot to tempt cross party cooperation to materialize, then it certainly met with a certain interest, as Field Marshal Methuen showed in writing to *The Times* on 28 January:

'...It is to be noted that each colony has adopted compulsory cadet training as its foundation. We worked on Lord Kitchener's admirable Australian scheme in forming the citizen army in South Africa.' [18]

Methuen was the ex-president of the National Defence Association which was in favour of a cadet force. He had sent a memorandum to Asquith on 26 February 1914 on the need for cadet training. Significantly, this very experienced soldier, who was very well regarded despite his less than stellar campaign in the Boer war, did not favour compulsion:

'My Dear Lansdowne
I forgot to say that the committee were unanimously against any compulsion when the lads reached 18. They believe they will join voluntarily. Let us hope they may.' [19]

The Conservative leaders were well aware that many of their followers regarded compulsion as antithetical to Conservatism for reasons which they shared, and as to how far the Conservatives were to go in cooperating with the government, there was confusion, as is apparent in this further extract from Curzon's memorandum:

'...Like Mr Long I am entirely against a Coalition government, even if (which I do not at present think in the least likely) it were proposed to us by the other side. A Coalition would tie our hands and close our lips more effectively than at present. It would make us responsible for many things that we ought to criticise, if not now, at any rate later: and with politicians so widely severed on almost all questions, save the war, as are the leading members of the two parties - it might lead to a disastrous breakdown followed by painful disclosures or injurious recriminations. If the country were actually and seriously invaded a Coalition government might become expedient and even necessary. But for the present it does not seem needful to discuss it.... (goes on to talk about conditions for cooperation with Gvt)...

A subsidiary but important feature would be an understanding with regard to the holding or postponement of the next General Election due at the end of this year. If the principle of some such clear understanding were accepted there are several ways by which it might be carried into effect...(goes on to talk of degree of responsibility to be enjoyed in return for cooperation)...Though I am a National Service man, I should be inclined not to cumber such a correspondence with any pronouncement or invitation about compulsory service, not because I doubt the propriety or patriotism of such a declaration but because I fear that while we shall have universal sympathy in attempting to define both our just obligations and our reasonable demands, we might alienate a portion of this sympathy if we were thought to be utilising the occasion to press forward a particular, or in some quarters unpalatable proposal, and might even retard its ultimate adoption by tempting the government to declare prematurely against it. [20]

He recognized that some sort of accommodation with the government would have to come, and that the necessity to postpone an election would bring it about. Yet how far this cooperation would go without some sort of coalition remained open to question. Why a coalition should be inevitable in the event of invasion, but not until, is not clear - the whole thing reads as rather woolly and vague. To Bonar Law and Lansdowne, their course was much more logical and very clear. Either they kept quiet with no responsibility, or if they wanted responsibility, then some sort of coalition was unavoidable. Since they did not, on the face of it, want coalition, patriotic opposition was the rational course to follow and in this they were in accord:

'...I rather think from your letter that your views are pretty much the same as my own in regard to this matter.' [21]

It is quite clear that the Conservatives, by the end of January 1915, were experiencing a division of opinion on the matter of compulsory service and that there was some discontent with the policy of the party leadership.

One thing that was not within their contemplation yet, though they spoke of it, was the notion of coalition because they evidently disagreed about it. Bentley Gilbert noted that Lloyd George approached Bonar Law and Austen Chamberlain about the possibility of a form of coalition government at the end of January; he wished them to sound Conservative opinion on the matter. They met on 26 January and Lloyd George took along with him a copy of his coalition proposition from 1910 but nothing came of it. The Conservative back-bench seemingly did not wish to speak of coalition but of pressing the government harder. Gilbert thought that Asquith was not told of this meeting, but at this date it is hard to see how Lloyd George could be approaching the Conservative leaders with even a tentative proposition of coalition unless Asquith did know of it. [22]

Walter Long's drive to change Conservative policy had not gone away, but he had now changed the direction of his manouevres. On 2 February 1915 a meeting was held of Unionist members in a committee room at the House of Commons. Many had been at the meeting with Walter Long the previous week where it had been decided to set up a Unionist Business Committee. Some accounts say that Bonar Law asked Walter Long to be chairman. In some newspapers however, it was reported that the MPs present elected Walter Long as its chief; he now had a formal power base with a very wide brief. In fact, Long so exercised Bonar Law's mind that he had 'placed' him in charge of the newly-founded and influential Unionist Business Committee. According to John Stubbs:

'Walter Long, who was the first chairman of the committee asserted that Bonar Law asked him to chair the committee...this was a shrewd move by Law to harness a restless Long to the development and harnessing of constructive criticism.' [23]

A shrewd move it might have seemed, but it may be that Bonar Law was simply confirming what had already happened to maintain the idea that he was in control. This places Long in the same committee as Professor WAS Hewins, a back bench MP and distinguished economist whom RJQ

Adams[24] presented as being prominent in a 'Ginger Group' which pressurized the government for a more effective prosecution of the war, and in May 1915 particularly. As the Chairman, and given his position in the party, it does not strain credibility to see Long as *L'Eminence Grise* behind this. When Long became a minister in May 1915 Hewins took over Chairmanship of the Unionist Business Committee (UBC). It is difficult to see Hewins as the dynamo behind this committee. He did not rise in the party as a result, never became a Minister, and quit Parliament in 1918 after failing to be re-elected. Long did make him Under Secretary for the Colonies, but he cut no figure in Parliament, at least one obituary in 1931 after his death stating that he was not a very effective Parliamentary debater. [25] Long employed him for his knowledge, for which he was respected, not his oratory which was not good, nor his charisma - he was Long's man. After this meeting, Long sent what RJQ Adams described rightly as a fiercely worded letter to Bonar Law. There is almost a sullen anger against the government doing whatever it wished to whilst facing no opposition:

'Here, not only has there been no Coalition - personally I do not favour it, and I gravely doubt its success- but the Government have persistently pursued those party aims which occupied them before the war.' [26]

Adams went on to show that Lord Curzon wrote similarly to Bonar Law on the same day complaining that the Liberals had all the advantages of a coalition whilst the Conservatives had all the drawbacks. It is quite clear that they wanted some sort of say in the running of the war. They might be chafing at the bit, but for the moment, in public at least, they toed the party line. This is perhaps why the Conservative Chief Whip Lord Edmund Talbot, began to attend the UBC at its second meeting to make sure they behaved themselves.

Lord Crewe's approaches as regards cadet training had evidently struck a chord too. The arch imperialist Sir George Goldie thought that the matter of cadet training could be placed above party politics:

'...best procedure in regard to obligatory military education of boys. ...The question might, as a result of these negotiations, be removed from the vicious circle of Politics and be treated as an entirely non-party question, as, I believe, the case was in Australia... I should imagine that Mr Asquith and Lord Lansdowne might come to an understanding.'[27]

Bridges between the parties could and were being built where they were allowed to take shape.

Walter Long was moderating his stance, in public at least; for the moment he heeded Lansdowne's request not to air the idea of compulsion - at least not in public. On 9 February he gave a long speech in the Commons on the subject of the numbers of men needed for the Army, but he studiously avoided the use of the compulsion word. He was unhappy about the uneven bearing of the national burden however and wished the government would take the House more into its confidence with facts and figures. His subtext was quite clear - he wished to see a more organized and national system of recruiting.[28] Whilst applauding what he said, *The Daily Record* of the following day found the debate as a whole 'brilliantly unilluminating.'

On the question of inoculation of troops, some of who had died from adverse reactions, Mr Long stated that he had the authority of the leader of the opposition for saying that they would give the government all the support which it was thought necessary to ensure the health of the army; for the moment and in public, the Conservatives sang from the same hymn sheet.

The *Aberdeen Evening Express* reported on 18 February that Mr Walter Long was laid up with influenza and confined to his house. Mr Long's health was never good, but for a week or so the driving force of compulsion on the Conservative Right was out of action. Bonar Law might have been excused, had he breathed a sigh of relief at a period of peace.

There was, of course, at this time no evidence at all that there was a shortage of men in the army. Recruiting was still steady whilst the Army was training every man it could get, and almost a miracle was being accomplished in their equipping and provisioning. Britain was acquiring an Army in a matter of a few short months on a scale hitherto undreamt of. They could not be sent to France untrained though, but that, too, was going on apace. Nonetheless, the government was alive to the problems of manpower, and the balance between Army and industry, as they discussed it on 22 February in response to a very long memorandum from Lloyd George.

He spelled out his fears that the enemy were out-producing the allies and that the British were not doing enough to fight the war in terms of either production or of numbers of men. He thought that Britain should be fielding an army of 3,500,000 instead of one of 2,000,000; nonetheless, he did not feel that compulsion was necessary in order to achieve it, as the men would come if made aware that their services were needed. He plainly felt that more effort was required in the conduct of the war. Evidently Kitchener had read this memorandum beforehand as he had prepared a reply. Kitchener thought that attrition would eventually force the Germans to sue for peace, he anticipated at the beginning of 1917. The crux of the situation was the organization of the skilled labour needed to work machinery; given that then he could envisage an army of 3,000,000 supported in the field.[29] Nonetheless there was a problem. John Burns, who was still helping out at the Local Government Board, despite his resignation from the Presidency, had already seen the problem in action, telling his diary on 5 February:

'LGB. Letters, interviews. Very little relief work. The fact is there is a shortage of men and soon will be a shortage of women for nearly all forms of productive work.'[30]

The unregulated enlistment of men into the army at the start of the war was having its effects.

A command report released in mid February showed that a staggering number of men had joined up and that its effects could not be ignored. Industry by industry the answers to enquiries showed that about one third of workers had joined the army. The coal industry was hit particularly hard as production was falling, and in some area over two thirds of bus crews had joined up.[31] If men continued to join up in an unregulated way then the industrial capacity of the United Kingdom, and its ability to fight a major war, were going to be hit very badly indeed; and what had been done so far was bad enough. Kitchener saw the problem plainly enough:

'...the real crux of the situation is, in my opinion, the organization of the skilled labour necessary to work the machinery...I have little doubt that in time an increased number of men, up to a total of 3,000,000 may be recruited and trained, fit to take the field. In the efforts we are now making to raise, arm and equip 2,000,000 men we are faced with grave difficulties, not the least of which is that, constantly our manufacturers find themselves, owing to shortage of skilled labour, to keep their promises of delivery of arms, ammunition etc...'[32]

He went on to say that some modifications in Trades Union rules were needed, but the great difficulty he foresaw was that of labour. The need to organize manpower in Britain had been flagged up quite clearly. The disruption to production caused by unregulated recruiting may be imagined. In some industries it was worse than others – in some coalfields 30% of miners had gone, and output of coal had gone down. A nation engaged in a great war needs to find the balance between production and numbers of soldiers; this had not been done.

Lord Willoughby de Broke, Conservative peer and in favour of compulsion, had another and very interesting idea at this time:

'... If I may say so I firmly believe that it is sound policy to make radical ministers commit themselves publicly on the general question of expanding our military resources. If they go with us, so much the better for them. If they shuffle, they will not be much loss. Their record, particularly in respect of Lord Haldane, is very bad. And there are indications that they still think that the vast mass of public opinion is as rotten as they have tried - and partially succeeded- in making it. I should feel happier if I thought that we were going to work at the military question without them. I suggest that we shall stand a very good chance of isolating the radical cancer from a good deal of its following and create a healthy public opinion on our own account..[33]*

This notion that it might be possible to isolate the Radical element of the Liberal Party from the more 'moderate' members, and thus creating a public opinion that was healthy, and by implication, cross party, demonstrates a certain move towards a coalition mentality. The Liberal right and the Conservative left might find common ground, to the exclusion of their more difficult elements. Nor can de Broke have been alone in this sentiment at this time because if he was talking about it, then it is a fair chance that others were too.

Trouble with the Law for the Law Family

On Monday 15 February David Mitchell, and John Law, two more Directors of Jacks & Co were arrested by the police in Scotland. Bail was set at £5,000 and they were released. John Law, known to his friends and family as Jack, was the beloved elder brother of Andrew Bonar Law, the leader of the Conservative Party. Bonar Law[34], was much distressed by the prosecution; and well might he be as it had the potential to end his career, tainted by the disgrace of trading with the enemy, and having money deposited in the company which had done so.

Prince Louis of Battenberg, the First Sea Lord, born German but naturalized Briton had been forced to resign in 1914 merely because of his origins, despite his acknowledged patriotism. RB Haldane, one of Asquith's closest political friends, was being pilloried in the Conservative press for having previously said that Germany was his spiritual home, and for having taken holidays in Germany before the war. The vivid imagination of Lord Northcliffe, owner of *The Times*, had the British government in December 1914 sheltering German spies in high places. In the hysterical anti-German mood of the time, the soaring casualties and rumours of conspiracy everywhere, the arrest of his elder brother must have brought Bonar Law up short.

Jack Law was questioned closely by the police and examined by the Procurator Fiscal of Glasgow, and his position was that his dealings as an actual executive of the company had ceased two years before and that he had no responsibility whatsoever for the day to day running of the company. The Procurator Fiscal service in Scotland, is the body that decides whether or not a prosecution should go ahead or not, and the Head of the Procurator Fiscal Service is the Crown Agent. The Crown Agent in 1915 was William Stowell Haldane, the brother of Lord Haldane, who was at this time the Lord Chancellor.

Arnold Rowntree, Liberal MP for York, was much taken by the news, writing home to his wife:

'...The chief item of news at the House was that Bonar Law's brother is charged with trading with the enemy- a particularly bad case- shipping ore for Krupps! He is at present out on bail. I doubt whether Bonar Law will be able to continue as leader if his brother is convicted- but the trial is not for some time yet....'[35]

Thus, the news was common knowledge in Parliament, yet no-one mentioned it in the House. Considering the treatment meted out to Liberals like Lloyd George over Marconi, and Haldane, there is a temptation to think there was some sort of ban in operation against raising the matter. Even in the press where it was mentioned, the name of the company was not, and reference was made to 'the four directors', and the name Law was certainly not mentioned at all. Although it was widely reported in newspapers that two accused had been seen by Sheriff Lyall in his chambers, behind closed doors and with no-one else present, the names of the accused were not given. They were the Glasgow merchants accused of trading with the enemy - just another such case and not uncommon at this time. [36]

As to why this was so, an article from *The Spectator* of 28 November 1914 on the policies being followed by the Director of the Press Bureau Stanley Buckmaster, appointed by Asquith in September, may shed some light:

'In his defence of his management of the Press Bureau last week Sir Stanley Buckmaster claimed a right under the Defence of the Realm Consolidation Bill to stop all criticism which" might destroy public confidence in the Government." A moment's consideration will suggest the abuses to which a general application of such a vague principle might lend itself. The Press Bureau might be used to hush up every blunder or folly of a Minister...'

This is very true, and Sir Stanley did indeed keep a very tight grip on what was allowed in print. The matter must have preyed on Bonar Law's mind somewhat though, as a letter from late March 1915 to Max Aitken, later Lord Beaverbrook, an old friend from Canada, may indicate:

'...There is nothing to write about. Politics were dead even while the House was sitting & are buried now. I have practically nothing to do & must be glad even of my old directorships to amuse me...' [37]

Quite aside from the rather strange and disingenuous statement that the leader of the Conservative Party had nothing to do, the fact that he was taking an interest in his old Directorships, which included Jacks & Co, indicates that his former connections might have been troubling him. The statement itself is most revealing, for Aitken was supposed to be one of Bonar Law's closest friends. It is absurd that when his brother has been arrested and charged with trading with the enemy, and that his own disgrace and the ruin of his political career have become possible, he should write that he had nothing to do and imply that he needed amusement; and if there was no speculation as to his successor within the Conservative Party, then their restraint was remarkable. Rowntree cannot have been the only person who doubted that the leader of the Conservative Party would be able to stay in his place if his brother was convicted. However, as Rowntree said, the trial was not to be for some time and Bonar Law's position, though shaky, would be safe enough until then. Nevertheless, if the wait and the stress of his job did not affect him, then he would be more than human. Certainly the arrest of his brother and the

70

forthcoming trial of his brother and three of his oldest friends and business acquaintances cannot have left him unaffected. He was not telling though and evidently, from the tone of his letter to Aitken, Bonar Law quite doggedly kept his own counsel.

Chapter 5

Coalition in the Air

On 8 March 1915 Lord Lansdowne received a letter from Asquith that stated:

'... I am strongly of opinion that the present attitude and future policy of this country should only be determined after consultation and in concert (my italics) with the responsible leaders of both parties. I therefore venture to hope that you may find it possible to attend a meeting of the War Council here on Wednesday next, the 10th at 11.30am. I am addressing a similar invitation to Mr Bonar Law.'[1]

Bonar Law's pencilled reply - 'I am obliged by your letter and in the circumstances I shall be pleased to attend the council on Wedy.'[2]

He was not too privileged, as Asquith had already told Venetia Stanley on 6 March the great secret to be discussed at the meeting. The situation that prompted this invitation was the proposed offering to the Russians of Constantinople in the event of victory. Asquith felt that this was a reversal in traditional British foreign policy, which indeed it was, and that the leaders of all parties were entitled to be involved in it, particularly as he might not be in office when victory came. He also felt that the party in government then would face difficulties over honoring a promise made by a previous administration. Participation by the opposition would also serve to convince the Russians that the offer was a good one, to be honoured by whichever party was in power. Ostensibly this was a good reason for the invitation, because it was a matter of national policy, not resource management or internal politics. The interests of social harmony, national efficiency and national unity made it important to involve the opposition. Yet if it is read again and out of the Russian context, it is about as clear an invitation as can be imagined to become involved in government decision-making. Nor was it to be the only rapprochement made in mid-March.

A bill for the disendowment of the Welsh Church had been postponed at the same time as Irish Home Rule in September 1914; business to be continued after the war. Yet it appeared that the Welsh Church Commissioners were taking preliminary steps towards disendowment. The Liberals put forward a bill to make the postponement complete if the Conservatives would agree not to impede the bill coming into force when the war was over. Lansdowne gave his assent and the bill was passed in the

Lords. When it came up for discussion in the Commons on 15 March Asquith made a:

'...quiet temporizing lubricating sort of speech...with the result that B Law was like heather honey, and gave me his benediction.' [3]

The Bill went forward, for the moment, with the support of both party leaders. It is quite clear that in some circumstances, cracks were present in the policy of non-cooperation; the case of Constantinople was a clear example.

Asquith did not have to consult over his policy towards Russia. He was Prime Minister and he had a majority; had he chosen to go ahead with the deal, with the current and legitimate mandate of the British people, albeit dating from 1910, then that agreement would have been binding on the next government of whatever party. It is more than plausible that he was actively seeking to bring in the Conservatives on this pretext, because it was such a big issue that it did not seem to be a pretext. If they were tempted it might be that it would give them a taste for participation and tempt them further yet, into actual coalition. However, it was still obvious that he had reservations about coalition when he told Venetia on 9 February that the French had a kind of coalition government of all the talents. Its members hated each other, afraid of everything, even their own shadow, and he did not think it had much backbone. Yet despite his ambivalence it must have seemed obvious that in Britain coalition would have advantages.

Churchill was later to write in *The World Crisis:*

'I had long wanted to see a national coalition formed. I viewed with great disquiet the spectacle of this powerful Conservative party brooding morosely outside, with excellent information from the services, and complete detachment from all responsibility.... We needed their aid. The Empire needed their aid....I had frequently talked to Mr Asquith in this sense...' [4]

This avowal, which Asquith referred to as 'W always hankering after coalitions' to Venetia on 9 February places it firmly in Asquith's mind. The Prime Minister's seeming determination to include members of the opposition in his government and in his counsels appears to bear out that he was actually seeking some form of coalition, but on his own terms. If so, then up to this point success had eluded him.

If the Constantinople invitation was aimed at such an end, then it fell on mostly stony ground. Bonar Law and Lansdowne did attend the meeting but sat, mostly mute like a pair of tailors' dummies to Asquith's mind – he was not impressed with the result of his invitation. However, they did turn up and this in itself signaled a willingness to cooperate even in such a vestigial fashion, but it seems that their participation was more interested than Asquith said. However Lewis Harcourt, Secretary of the colonies, was also attending that meeting, keeping a diary he was not supposed to keep, and his diary entry gives rather a different impression to Asquith's interpretation to Venetia:

Balfour; We must give Russia Constantinople, but I don't like it. Let us get the best we can in exchange.
Asq and Kitch. Mentioned Alexandretta.
Bonar Law and Lansdowne rather inclined to give Russia no pledge as to Constantinople at present, but in the end agreed to our views.' [5]

The meeting sent a message to the Russians to the effect that Britain was willing to assent to the Russians getting the straits and Constantinople provided that Britain and France got a substantial share of the carcase (*sic*) of the Turk. If Bonar Law and Lansdowne did not say much, it also has to be said that Asquith, by his own admission was very silent himself and let Grey and Balfour do most of the talking. If Harcourt is to be believed, however, Bonar Law and Lansdowne had found common ground on an important policy with Asquith and agreed a course to be followed; this was, as in a coalition, a joint decision. It is perhaps a great pity that this sort of cooperation did not continue over policy towards Constantinople, because it might conceivably have altered the course of the war, had Asquith faced an effective opposition case at the next meeting in the following week. Giving Russia no pledge after the first meeting would have left the Government's hands free to negotiate with the Turks more freely. On 15 March, two British agents, George Eady and Edwin Whittall, met Turkish representatives with the object of buying Turkey out of the war. According to the diary of Maurice Hankey, the Cabinet Secretary, they had been authorized to offer £4,000,000; and the Turks considered it very seriously.[6] Many Turks did not wish to be at war with Britain, and the only thing that halted the negotiations on 19 March was the agents' inability to guarantee that Constantinople would be Turkish when the war ended. If the negotiations had succeeded, then the British supply route through the Black Sea to Russia would have been open and the course of history would have been altered. A meeting that had decided to do as Lansdowne and Bonar Law had suggested, would have given no undertaking to Russia after the meeting of 10 March, and the agent's hands would have been free to give the Turks the guarantee they wished for. In retrospect, the decision of the War Council undermined the mission of the agents, which was already under way; they would have done better to have waited. That Balfour was taking such a marked part in the proceedings of the meeting cannot have been lost on the Conservative leader. Nor can it have been lost that the Conservative advice that held the stronger weight in the War Council was not theirs, but Balfour's.

Five days later however, on 15 March, Bonar Law put an end to any speculation that he might attend more meetings by telling Asquith that he and Lansdowne could not attend any more such meetings without weakening their support in their own party and therefore their ability to help the government.[7] So even if they had been free to rescind the message given to the Russians about Constantinople, the Conservatives would not be attending any more meetings anyway. The last part of the message was at least an indicator that Bonar Law was not unwilling to help. Indeed according to Hankey, Bonar Law told Asquith that he had 'thoroughly enjoyed' the meeting and profited from it. As a result of this remark, Asquith instructed Hankey that in future he was to not invite Mr Bonar Law and Lord Lansdowne to the War Council, but that he must send them all papers prepared for the Council.

This was a coalition offer manqué, and Hankey found it almost beyond his belief:

'How astonishing is the influence of party politics'[8]

Bonar Law's move was prompted solely by anger within the Conservative ranks, which had been forcefully put by Walter Long even before the meeting of the War Council in a Commons speech of 11 March.[9] He referred to the government having thanked opposition members for the help they had given since the beginning of the war, but pointed out some words of Bonar Law in which he described the situation as a 'farce'. The Tories helped, but were not consulted, got no recognition for their help, and the Government did what it wanted in an almost dictatorial way. The Conservative party had laid its weapons aside and not forced any divisions and all they could do was urge their views on the House, which the government ignored. Long deplored the lack of a Committee to oversee the conduct of the war and criticized roundly the organization of the government in many areas. He pressed the government to state how many men it wanted for the Army and spoke of the hopeless failure of the recruiting system. It was a very long speech, ranged widely, and criticized the conduct of the war on a number of headings. In short, it was the sort of speech that could and should be made by a man fitted to lead a great political party. There was something else.

In the House the previous day, Bonar Law had spoken and had touched on the subject of the War Office giving compensation to people whose property was used by the army; he told a tale of a friend of his who had been very angry because the compensation offered by the Army had not been enough.

In his speech, Walter Long mentioned a farmer he knew who had tried to charge the War Office a large amount of money for spoiling his turnip field - but Long had been there and told the War Office representative that the 'damage' amounted to a few pounds – the farmer was trying it on. That what Long said undermined what Bonar Law had said, in the most innocent way of course, cannot have been lost on the Conservative leader.[10]

Thomas Gibson Bowles, journalist, former Conservative, then Liberal MP, but now returned to the Conservatives, was very impressed, and it may be assumed that his sentiments were not isolated:

'Let me heartily congratulate you on your speech of yesterday. It is most important that some leader of the historic Conservative Party should affirm and exercise the duty of an opposition when such things are being done as we now see. The country has a right to that and without that Parliament ceases to be.'[11]

In the stinging implication that their leaders were not speaking out as they should, and that Long was filling that need, lay danger for Bonar Law. He appeared to his back-benchers to sit, like King Log in Aesop's fable, whilst Long spoke for the party; he was, of course, very popular. And Balfour sat in the War Council.

JL Garvin, the editor of The Observer, wrote a leading article on 21 March on 'The Temper of the Nation':

'The Nation for the first time is uneasy about the Government and itself. It believes in some individual Ministers like Mr Lloyd George and Mr Churchill, Lord Kitchener and Sir Edward Grey, but it distrusts a purely

Party Cabinet framed with no view to the efficient conduct of the war in the greatest of world crises, and it is beginning to doubt whether we have at the head the strong directing, yet unifying force which is a prime requisite for the supreme vigour of our effort and the triumph of our arms.'

This scarcely veiled highlighting of the desirability of unity, or coalition, from a leading Conservative journalist was not shared by all in his party, save with grave reservations HA Gwynne, the editor of the *Morning Post* who wrote to Bonar Law on 26 March, evidently disturbed by what he had been hearing on the subject of coalition.[12] He said first of all that there had been talk for some time of a coalition government, and he thought it had to be considered from the point of view of the nation's welfare, and the Party's welfare. The government alone was responsible for the carrying on of the war, and any request for a coalition had to come from them. Only they could judge if they needed help, otherwise the Conservative party must just pledge loyal support of the war effort. If a coalition offer did not include some of the high offices like Chancellor of the Exchequer, Admiralty, War Office Treasury or Colonial Office then it would help the government but limit the influence of the Conservatives in influencing the war. He also did not wish to see the Liberals fragment and set up an 'anti-war party'. The government however, had given up to Lord Kitchener powers which they should have kept in their own hands, and a coalition might not actually help in such a situation:

'It may be argued that it would be unreasonable to expect that a government which after all is a party government, should go to an opposition and make a confession of weakness. My answer to that is that they are the sole judges of the needs of the present situation especially as regards the war, and if they think that the war can be brought to a successful conclusion only by the active help of the opposition, it is their bounden duty to say so.'[13]

The disadvantages of a coalition, for Gwynne, outweighed the advantages, especially in the absence of a settlement of Ireland and the Welsh Church problems; a coalition that did not solve these would weaken the Conservatives and might break up the Liberal Party; and both of these effects would be disastrous for the country, as the opposition would then consist of the Labour Party socialists and the extreme left of the Liberal Party:

'It is not for the Conservative Party to get into power by any means. That is not the only aim and object of the Party. Its aim is to carry out those principles to which it is pledged, and any coquetting with the government in the hope of securing a few offices, would irretrievable destroy the party... '[14]

He thought Bonar Law's current attitude of patriotic opposition admirable and very good for stirring the government up without getting tied into a coalition, which would limit what they could do. Bonar Law was trapped into immobility and his party was split down the middle with Long wanting action now. When Lloyd George told Margot that the opposition was 'longing for a coalition...'[15] he was not speaking of Long but of Bonar Law - he meant half of the opposition.

Balfour was not merely 'sitting in' on the War Council either. Towards the end of March 1915 Edwin Montague, newly appointed to the Cabinet as Chancellor of the Duchy of Lancaster, told Asquith that Balfour was gaining an 'hypnotic ascendancy' over Lloyd George and Churchill and that Winston Churchill had suggested that Balfour be put in charge of the Foreign Office, whilst Edward Grey went on a holiday he was taking for his health.[16] He was functioning almost as a minister too, working on the War Munitions Committee, helping to draft replies to President Wilson protesting about violations of neutrality on US ships, preparing a memorandum on cordite for the navy, studying a report on the defences of Constantinople and advising against a landing at Gallipoli. He also set to examining the problem of drink affecting productivity, preparing a memorandum on the subject for the Cabinet, and recommended banning all drink except with meals. He was a one man working paradigm of coalition in action.

March to April 1915

On 22 March, Asquith spoke to Venetia in the stress and tumult of a controversy on the subject of munitions supply involving Lloyd George, Balfour and Churchill that was wordy and windy. The ex-Conservative Prime Minister was involved in a range of activities and discussions at ministerial level. Asquith met all of them, with Montague, and they agreed to take the contracts for war munitions out of Kitchener's hands and put them into the hands of a new Cabinet Committee with Lloyd George at its head. This was a very important decision for an outsider to be involved in; evidently Balfour had formed his own 'coalition". Ironically this controversy appears to have been sparked off by Kitchener himself who had complained at the Cabinet meeting of 19 March that too much ammunition had been wasted at Neuve Chappelle. 114,000 shells had been fired which was more than during the whole of the Boer war. Nor was this the only way in which Balfour was now at the centre of things; here at least was one Conservative to whom some Liberals were getting very close.

Geoffrey Robinson, the Editor of *The Times* wrote to Lord Esher on 22 March:

'We shall come before long to a National Cabinet for the simple reason that the present Cabinet dare not take the necessary action on their own account. Perhaps it may be all the better to have such a change now that we know all our mistakes, though I always think that the PM was a fool, from his own point of view, not to do it from the beginning'[17]

This ignores utterly that a coalition from the beginning was an utter impossibility, though was courted during August 1914 and rejected by Bonar Law in his walkout in September 1914. Even if Asquith wanted a coalition, he could not have had one in the face of the Conservative policy of 'patriotic opposition',

On 24 March Massingham, editor of *The Nation* told Margot Asquith at lunch with Asquith[18] that Churchill was intriguing hard to get Edward Grey replaced at the Foreign Office by Balfour; and also that he told Balfour rather too many things which would be best kept within the Cabinet. As Asquith told Venetia, he asked Lloyd George if the story was true and the Chancellor thought that it was. In the minds of some ministers it appears the party lines were beginning to melt. It was a strange position that Balfour was in where he was in the War Council, virtually a Committee of the Cabinet, privy to all sorts of things that the Cabinet was not, yet he was not in the Cabinet.

This became the implicit subject of some discussion in Cabinet on 26 March[19] when Jack Pease, the Education Secretary and Herbert Samuel, President of the Local Government Board raised the subject of Parliamentary registration. There would have to be an election before the end of the year, or by January 1916, as the mandate of the government would run out. The electorate was exclusively male, and hundreds of thousands of them were serving abroad, whilst many more were on the move as industry geared up to war and new factories opened. If some sort of accurate register for an election were to be compiled, then the work must be started. Lloyd George said that he thought the election should be postponed by involving the Parliament Act of 1911. It is easy to see why - organizing and holding any sort of meaningful election during a great war would be an horrendous task. Lewis Harcourt the Colonial Secretary was against it on the grounds that he could not see the Parliament Act being used for this purpose, so early into its existence. But Lord Crewe, Liberal leader in the Lords, said quite clearly that coalition was one course open to them as the price for an agreement with the opposition to postpone an election, which Lloyd George thought 'improbable'. Charles Hobhouse, the Postmaster General, then included this sentence in his diary entry for that day:

'Whereat McK, WR, and I winked knowing what he and WSC and we believe K had been up to, and the reason Balfour had been admitted to the Labour conferences against our general wish. The PM remarked that he could not believe the Opposition wished to have any responsibility for the conduct of the war' [20]

McKenna the Home Secretary, Walter Runciman at the Board of Trade, and Hobhouse himself were very shrewd men, well organized and good at what they did. Obviously they had been against the inclusion of Balfour as a member of the newly created Cabinet Munitions of War Committee. Kitchener was trying to outflank moves by Lloyd George to take over the supply of munitions by bringing in outside experts and retaining control of munitions supply at the War Office. Asquith may have been damping down speculation about the idea of coalition as some in his Cabinet would not like the idea, but if the inclusion of Balfour had been against the 'general wish' then the only way he can have been included was at the Prime Minister's insistence. It is strange for a man to say that he is against coalition, then over-ride the views of his own party colleagues to place a leading member of the opposition into a position of power and influence.

The end of March 1915 was a crucial time for Asquith because it signaled the end of the honeymoon period for his government that had existed since the declaration of war. It took some time to become apparent, but by the end of March it was clear that the Battle of Neuve Chapelle, in the Western Front, had been a debacle. As the extent of this became clearer over the next month, the relationship between the Prime Minister and his Commander in the field in France was to undergo a significant change. In addition to this, the government, the navy and the army, had invested much

80

time in attacking the Dardanelles in an attempt to capture Constantinople. This also had suffered a humiliating reverse – and over the next few weeks *The Times* was to portray this as a disaster. Innuendoes in and out of the press were beginning to circulate that Asquith was not up to his job and that someone more dynamic might be better at number 10. Lloyd George had been receiving a deal of praise in the Northcliffe newspapers, and had also been adding fuel to the fire himself. Asquith's disdain of the press was not helpful here; on 29 March he actually told Venetia that he was indifferent to press criticism and did not care one damn about it. Lloyd George, on the other hand socialized with and took into his confidence a number of eminent newspapermen including CP Scott of the *Manchester Guardian*, William Robertson Nicoll of the *British Weekly*, and especially George Riddell of the *News of the World*, with whom he often played golf. He flattered them by seeking their opinions and giving them the impression that they were his trusted advisors and that their opinions had great weight. On 13 March Riddell had asked Lloyd George is the war was being conducted with sufficient vigour, and he answered:

'Things are very unsatisfactory in that respect'.[21]

Curiously, the Chancellor thought that Asquith needed to take a firmer control on departments instead of just letting them do their own thing. At any rate, when Asquith, in response to the circulating rumours, tackled him about any intrigues against him, Lloyd George on 29 March told him that he would break stones, dig potatoes or be hanged drawn and quartered before he would do an act, say a word, or harbour a thought that was disloyal to the Prime Minister - and wrung his hands, eyes wet with tears. Asquith thought him sincere despite the fact that Lloyd George had again told his favourite newspaper editor the day before that the machine (of government) wanted more guidance; Asquith was evidently amused when he described this scene to Venetia. Curiously, when Lloyd George reported this conversation to George Riddell the following day it was Asquith who was in tears in his version; Riddell thought that the Welshman looked ill. It is unlikely that the Prime Minister was in tears, as he appears to have had foreknowledge of the rumours about intrigues, as Hobhouse told his diary on 21 April of a discussion he had with Walter Runciman about plots against the Prime Minister:

'We discussed the PM who is aware of all these movements through his jackal Montague, who howls in sympathy with any camp.' [22]

Montague, shortly to marry Venetia Stanley, was Asquith's protégé, newly appointed to the Cabinet in February 1915, and he owed his promotion and prospects to Asquith. It would in his interests to keep his chief, whom he seems to have revered sincerely, well informed.

Asquith made a serious mistake in what seemed a small matter on 30 March. Lloyd George, convinced that drunkenness was hitting production in factories, wanted to launch a campaign against drink, and on this day the Cabinet received an offer from the King to abstain from all drink for the duration of the war and to ban it in the Royal household. The Cabinet accepted this offer as setting an example worthy to follow for the nation, but Asquith himself did not take the pledge, preferring to have a drink when he wished. The casual nickname of 'Squiff' which had been applied to him on occasion before now, soon came into common circulation and damaged his reputation as the press campaign against him over the next year heated up. The subject of drink was to provide Asquith with some interest in the next few days.

After the Cabinet he had an interview with Reginald McKenna, the Home Secretary, and Lloyd George, Chancellor of the Exchequer, on the subject of the intrigue against him. McKenna had accused Lloyd George of being behind it. Churchill was invited too but did not come, stating that he had confidence in the Prime Minister to represent him; Asquith took that as a sign of great loyalty. McKenna and Lloyd George disliked each other and the expected histrionic row took place with loud accusations and denials, but Asquith reconciled them with an uncharacteristic bombshell:

'Very well; in another week I shall have sat in this chair for 7 years. If I have the slightest reason to think that there is anyone among you who has even the faintest doubt or suspicion about me, I will gladly (for what have I to gain or lose?) abandon this chair and never sit in it again.' [23]

This stunned them into resolving their own quarrel and telling Asquith that the day he left, they too would disappear, never to return. They were right - the disgrace of having brought Asquith down at this time would have finished the person who did it. Even if Lloyd George had wished to supersede Asquith at this time, the time was not ripe and the fact of the matter was that at that moment there was simply no-one able to replace him; no-one capable of being the buckle on the strap that held the Liberal Party together or of being able to command an unquestioned majority in the house.

The end of March was a significant turning point for another reason too. Lord Crewe, the Liberal leader in the Lords was a man much esteemed by Asquith for his intellect, and considered by him to be one of the Cabinet's top rank brains, the others being McKenna, Lloyd George, and Churchill. It seems that Crewe had been speaking to some Conservatives about the idea of compulsory cadet training, which had first been mooted in the Lords at the end of January. This cannot have been done without Asquith being consulted, because a proposition has no weight if it cannot be delivered. The Conservative compulsionists were interested in this form of compulsion as a possible way forward; indeed some of their members had been pressing for it for years, as members of the National Service League (NSL). Bonar Law evidently did not think that this idea could be delivered, not because of Asquith, but because it would face opposition from the Liberal left. Lord Scarborough, who was in favour of the scheme, wrote to Lansdowne on 20 March:

'...if Bonar Law's view is correct, that the government would be afraid to face the hostility of radical members, then our whole object would be defeated and Crewe's blessing would be of no practical effect'[24]

Scarborough seems to have received an assurance from Crewe, that the Liberal leaders would not oppose a cadet scheme in principle. It was enough for Scarborough to write to Sir George Goldie urging that Lord Willoughby de Broke, who was intent on forcing a scheme through the Lords, should 'hold his hand' so that:

'...we should avoid the risks of precipitate action...'

and to send a copy of the letter to Lansdowne.[25]

It is evident that some of the Tory leaders at least were being tempted into further cooperation with the Government. Goldie too shared this view, as he had written to Lansdowne on 21 March obviously quite willing to be tempted:

'...the only solution seems to be that Asquith should be sounded. I have undoubted authority for saying that he is <u>personally</u> in favour of our plan.'[26]

Goldie may well have borne in mind that some form of compulsory service was one of the concessions offered to the Conservatives in 1910, when Lloyd George was attempting to entice them into a coalition. Goldie also thought it likely that if the government signified its support, then

Kitchener would lend his weight to putting the scheme into action. According to Goldie, Bonar Law was still wary at this stage, doubting that Asquith would find the time to listen to Goldie for fear of his own radicals, whom Lansdowne tactfully referred to as 'Parliamentary difficulties.' Indeed any concession on compulsion would be a major compromise with Liberal ideology and could cause great disquiet in the party. Yet this was exactly why Crewe cannot possibly have made the offer without consulting Asquith; certainly it revealed another avenue for cross party cooperation.

It was doubtful though that Kitchener would back conscription willingly, for he did not like it on the grounds that it did not produce very good quality troops. His belief might well have been reinforced by the receipt of a memorandum earlier in the year from Lord Hardinge, Viceroy of India which cast grave doubt on the quality of the Territorial troops that had been sent out to India as garrison to replace Regulars who had gone to war – they were apparently of:

'very small military value'. [27]

Asquith was not in any danger from Liberal radicals at this stage of the war. There certainly was opposition to compulsion among the Liberal back benches, but the left wing of the party was not united in any coherent force, and the right wing discontent of later in the war had not yet appeared. Nonetheless, if Asquith *appeared* to be moving towards compulsion or even seeking coalition with the Conservatives it could serve to unite his radicals against such a move and threaten his position, especially if such controversial issues as compulsion in any form came onto the government's list of policy aims. That the Liberal radical threat to Asquith was not a chimera has been well established by Trevor Wilson:

'The Party was profoundly shaken in May 1915 by his decision…to form a Coalition ministry; it required a twenty-minute exhortation from him to dissuade a meeting of over a hundred Liberal MPs from passing a resolution hostile to the change. On this occasion he warned them quite frankly that if the resolution was adopted he would leave office. The same threat, even if not explicitly repeated, faced his followers whenever they felt like challenging his authority.' [28]

By Asquithian standards this was a brutal and authoritarian threat, not often used - but he did use it occasionally, and indicates quite plainly his determination to force accommodation with the Conservatives on his party whether it wanted it or not. It also shows the strength he had at his disposal if he chose not to go for coalition; he did not have to do it.

So in late March 1915 there was a caucus of Conservatives who thought it likely that Asquith was in favour of their plans for a cadet force, and not against it on principle - some even displayed a certain sympathy for him - there is even a note of fellow-feeling in the letters for a Prime Minister willing to compromise on a matter they gave importance to, yet forced into a position by his own side where he could not listen.

On their side the Conservative leaders were, with some difficulty containing their own radicals who were intent on bringing compulsion in by changing policy to something the leadership did not want. Walter Long, Willoughby de Broke, Professor Hewins and Arthur Steel Maitland were the tip of a very large group who might force a leadership struggle in the party. This divide caused great dissension in the party between the anti-compulsionists of Bonar Law and the pro-compulsionists whose chief spokesman was emerging as Walter Long.

The Liberal and Conservative leadership had thus found at least one piece of common ground; they were both against the immediate implementation of conscription. Asquith's achievement in bringing this about was a significant one in party politics. The mood is caught in a letter from Lansdowne to Goldie on 23 March:

'Crewe's promise of a 'general blessing' was certainly not given without previous consultation with the Prime Minister, but it does not follow that, assuming Asquith to be, as you suppose, in favour of some such plan as yours, he will risk a troublesome discussion in the House of Commons at a moment when HM government are not unnaturally endeavouring to evade Parliamentary difficulties...I see no reason why you should not ask Asquith to see you and I have no objection whatever to your referring to my communications with Crewe...[29]

Quite apart from the obvious point that Lansdowne was disposed towards compromise with Asquith, it is significant to note that he had by now been tempted into talking to Crewe about the issue, and the matter was not solely a back-bench preoccupation. He was also quite understanding of why the government should wish to avoid difficulties in Parliament - they had other things to do that were more important. That the Conservative front bench leaders were disposed to compromise brought dividends to

Asquith. Lansdowne was of course in communication with many compulsionists. On 3 April he wrote to Bonar Law:

'..I have toned down my answer to Mr Salter (as to universal training) but in view of the possibility of a motion in the Lords and of the line which I have always taken, I do not think I could discourage Mr Salter and his friends from ventilating the question.[30]

His reluctance to push the issue is obvious, even though he could not restrain hotter heads in his party, but that very reluctance served Asquith's ends perfectly. Arthur Salter was among a number of otherwise unremarkable Conservative MPs now agitating for some form of compulsion and shaping up for a back-bench revolt on the issue with Walter Long at its head. Salter did not 'ventilate' the question, at least not in the Commons, but that Lansdowne and Bonar Law were under pressure from their own party over this issue, pushed them inexorably towards dialogue with the Liberals if they were not to concede over compulsion. The Prime Minister may not have been over-optimistic on 8 April when he wrote to the King after a cabinet meeting:

'... some discussion took place on the expediency of postponing registration and the election for another year and it was agreed to enter into communication with the opposition leaders on the subject.[31]

Since the Conservative leaders were already cautious about causing the government difficulties over compulsion, it may not have seemed unreasonable that they would be willing to be as considerate over the forthcoming election. One could hardly imagine a greater disruption to a country in a large-scale general war than a general election and it is sure that the Conservatives would wish to avoid the odium of having brought one about when they could have reached a compromise. After all, who would vote for a party that had shown such unpatriotic spirit and refused to help prosecute the war? Given that an individual's franchise lapsed after being abroad for twelve months, the time was coming when many serving soldiers would lose their votes. Asquith knew that there would be a price for postponing the election and maintaining the life of a parliament whose mandate had expired; the Conservatives would wish to have a say in government - that was only logical. Given their desire to preserve unity then their entry into coalition, if no election took place, was inevitable. That the coalition would be Liberal dominated, given the state of the parties in the house at that time, was obvious. However, the Conservatives would wish to see in that coalition those Liberals they felt they could work with; Asquith's indicators over the cadet scheme had made it clear yet again that he was quite congenial to working with Conservatives on issues of national interest:

'Coalition is in the air; there it will remain. If the war is going well, government will not share by coalition the credit with the opposition. If going badly opposition will leave misfortune to government.[32]

So wrote John Burns on 28 March, but he was not looking ahead far enough. The impending election made it impossible for the Conservative front bench to stay with Bonar Law's non-cooperation policy; they had to move off the fence especially if they wished to regain control of their own backbenchers. For the Conservatives to force an election was out of the question, given the numbers of MPs in the house. The Liberal and Conservative parties were evenly balanced, but Labour and Irish Nationalists voted with Asquith, so to form a Conservative government was impossible. However reluctantly, even unconsciously, they were moving towards participating in a Liberal dominated coalition; by his willingness to consider a small measure of compulsion Asquith was offering himself as the acceptable leader of what may quite aptly be described as a coalition of front benches.

Some of the Conservatives certainly did not wish it, as is clear from a letter from Lady Charles Beresford to HA Gwynne of the *Morning Post* early in April:

'Those devils are starting rumours of a Coalition government. Are we as stupid as that? Our worst enemy is AB who is always at the Asquith's and now has a room at Whitehall[33]

Discontent then, was simmering nicely within the Conservative Party, rumours were flying round of coalitions, Balfour's machinations, and of course, whether Bonar Law would be leader after his brother's trial.

The affair of the Themis, Jacks & Co and the shipment of ore traded with the enemy, had not faded away. Unfortunately, a letter from GH Robb of GH Robb & Crosbie, Bonar Law's solicitor in Glasgow, was not dated except 'Thursday' so its place in the sequence of events is lost:

'I am very sorry to say that the affair, notwithstanding all our efforts, is not well, and I am very much afraid a prosecution is inevitable… I have taken other step - perfectly discreet- to bring pressure on Munro and there is still

hope, but not much. I fear the temptation for Munro and his satellites to be in the limelight will be too strong for them...[34]

Despite efforts in the background then, the case against the directors of Jacks & Co was not going away. Robert Munro, the Lord Advocate, was to lead the prosecution for the Crown. Clearly attempts had been made in the background to persuade him not to proceed; also clear is that he had some discretion in the matter. 'Perfectly discreet' they might be, but plainly the Jacks case was being subjected to political manouevres and Bonar Law was involved. It might be possible to view him as being detached from events, as he was far away from Glasgow and he would not be in the dock at the trial- but his brother would be, the directors of his family firm would be, and his honour and reputation would be touched by it. Furthermore he had the solicitor handling the court case communicating with him directly- and not just any solicitor either. GH Robb and Crosbie of 30 George Square, Glasgow, with a swanky office of outstanding architectural merit were of high renown and among the best in Scotland at the time.

Munro and his satellites, who were of Liberal hue may have wanted their day in the limelight, but the limelight was not to be provided by their prosecuting a case of Trading with the Enemy. These were fairly commonplace. The limelight was to come from the *dramatis personae* in the dock, amongst whom was to be John Richard Kidston Law, iron and steel merchant of Glasgow. This letter is significant in the narrative leading to the formation of the May coalition in that it lifts the corner of what appears to be a very convoluted affair going on in Glasgow. Robb was reporting to a client; not Jack Law but Bonar Law. So the matter of his involvement is not in question because he certainly was involved. That his solicitor had taken steps to bring pressure onto the Lord Advocate takes on more possible significance if the nature of the Lord Advocate is taken into consideration. Robert Munro was the Liberal MP for Wick Burghs and the Lord Advocate was one of Scotland's Officers of State appointed by the Prime Minister when allocating offices in government.

There has to be a certain logic that if a man is involved directly in a serious court case, it will be a weight on his mind. If that man is a politician in a high position with much at stake, both politically and personally, then the weight of it must be considerable. Whatever else may be said, with this going on, on top of all other things happening round him, the mind of Bonar Law can hardly have been a smooth pond around the end of March 1915, and indeed in the week and months following.

Chapter 6

Of Drink, Coalition and Compulsion

On 1 April 1915 Lloyd George and Reginald McKenna were again in conclave with Asquith with a scheme to buy out the drinks industry and control it at a cost of £250 millions.[1] Lloyd George thought that drunkenness was affecting war production in factories and should be controlled. They had not really thought it through but Asquith and they all agreed that it would be useless without the cooperation of the Tories, if such a thing were to happen. Lloyd George announced that he would spend his Easter holiday trying to reconcile the warring factions - and in fact did speak to Bonar Law about it. On 7 April he told the Cabinet[2] that he was consulting the opposition of whom Bonar Law was 'friendly certainly'. Bonar Law, a teetotaler, thought that the Tory party being tied to the drinks trade did them more harm than good and thought Lloyd George's scheme 'a great reform'. He also stated that the Tory party would not oppose the proposal.[3] Another measure of accommodation had been reached - it appeared that the leading Conservatives and the leading Liberals could work very well together. Bonar Law and Lloyd George were now on the most friendly terms personally if not politically, which was perhaps unsurprising, both being from middle class backgrounds, having no aristocratic connections and having not been to a great public school. However, Bonar Law had not consulted his party on this matter, and many Conservative MPs were against the idea,[4] and particularly, as RJQ Adams pointed out, many members of the Unionist Business Committee, whose leader was Walter Long, although Long himself was in favour of the scheme. Bonar Law had in fact made rather a large mistake, as he was to find out over the next few weeks.

On Thursday 8 April Lloyd George was back at number 10 telling Asquith again about his great scheme for buying out the drinks industry and nationalizing it. He had been speaking to opposition leaders, temperance leaders, labour leaders, etc and securing cross-party agreement to his idea, underscoring yet again that Liberals were willing to bring other ideas into their counsels and that other parties were willing to work with the government across ideological and political divides. Asquith had given him his head on this but on 14 April he, Crewe and McKenna agreed that it was a chimera; he did not have to break it to Lloyd George because before he had a chance to do so, Lloyd George, who had evidently sensed opposition welling against the idea, presented him with an alternative for restrictions on drink in munition and camp areas, which was much more reasonable. [5] He had already admitted to George Riddell on 2 April that he did not favour total prohibition, when Riddell told him he thought it would be very dangerous.[6] Which it was - Keir Hardie thundered that Lloyd George had maligned the working classes by saying they were drunken wasters, which did nothing for the Chancellor's popularity. Lloyd George had also dined that day with the editors of the *Daily News, Daily Chronicle, Manchester Guardian, Liverpool Post and Westminster Gazette,* as you do if you are a government minister, and had proposed to them the buying out by the government of the drinks trade for £300,000,000, and all thought it a good idea save the *Daily Chronicle.* It was demonstrably quite possible to manufacture a consensus across the political divide, even with newspaper editors. Lloyd George did not tell Riddell, to whom he reported this meeting, that the scheme was now dead. Instead, eventually the Cabinet decided to raise taxes on drink as a means of raising revenue and decreasing consumption by increasing the cost.

On 18 April the Scottish Conservative Whip, Sir George Younger, himself a brewer wrote to Lloyd George telling him not to trouble to discuss the matter of nationalizing drink in Cabinet because unless they nationalized the breweries as well as the pubs:

'...no Unionist leader would ever dream of looking at such a scheme for a moment.'[7]

Here then was another matter that divided Bonar Law from much of his party; he had told Lloyd George that his party would not oppose measures to control drink, but he could not actually deliver on that promise. He had not been wise; 19 out of 23 MPs listed as having interests in the brewing industry, were Conservatives and five of them were active within the UBC of which Walter Long was Chair. It appears that Sir George Younger was Bonar Law's own personal 'link' with the UBC, so his backing for any banning of drink had probably irritated one of his closest supporters. However much he might have liked to cooperate with the government more closely in running the war, if his party did not wish to go where he wished to lead, then there was nothing seemingly, that he could do about it.

Asquith may not have liked the idea of coalition. Indeed, it is well known that he hated it. However, merely because he did not like the idea did not mean that he would not accept it or even seek to bring one into being, because he was a pragmatist, and probably saw a coalition as likely to prove more efficient in managing a war. The mere fact that Lloyd George had found consensus on the issue smoothed the way towards other accommodations; coalition approached inexorably.

Asquith's own government was so riven with faction and personal dislikes that it was something of a coalition in itself, and a classic example of this occurred on Friday 16 April during a meeting of the Cabinet. Kitchener had been enraged that figures he had given in confidence to the Cabinet about the size of the armies had been revealed in the Munitions Committee by Lloyd George. He declared that he could no longer be responsible for the War Office and tendered his resignation, rising from his chair, about to leave. Lloyd George and Churchill both took aggressive and very loud stances to this, but Edward Grey stood up for Kitchener, to Lloyd George's chagrin. Reginald McKenna was almost openly gloating about the imminent wreck of Lloyd George's committee, which he had always disliked, and it looked as if the government would fall - it could not have survived the resignation of Kitchener. Asquith, who had not the slightest warning of all this, pulled himself together, telling Venetia:

'...and by dint of appeals & warnings & gives & takes & all sorts of devices & expedients succeeded in getting us back into more or less smooth water and clear air...' [8]

During this altercation Lloyd George had made some injurious and wounding innuendoes about Kitchener, which Asquith did not disclose, but which he thought Kitchener would be more than human to forget. Smoothing the way was what Asquith did best and how he saw his role. His department chiefs did their jobs; his job was to do exactly what he had just done and keep the ship of state on course. As Maurice Hankey observed of this altercation:

'It required all Asquith's dexterity to avoid an open breach between his warring colleagues.' [9]

Nonetheless, the row shook Asquith, and he talked it over later with Crewe, whose judgment he rated highest among his colleagues; both of them felt disillusioned with their colleagues and depressed at the exhibition they had just witnessed. On 17 April he told Margot[10] that it was the saddest and most disagreeable meeting in his term of office. He thought Kitchener had meant what he said and came out of the row best. Churchill he thought bad, but as for Lloyd George and McKenna, he said to Venetia that it would be a very long time before he forgot and forgave their attitude. He did not often speak to Venetia in this way, but there is little doubt that he had revised his estimate of some of his colleagues, and for the worse, which depressed him. He saw the patched-up row as a slumbering volcano, and the truce between Lloyd George and Kitchener as the thinnest and most precarious kind. In the Cabinet of 19 April he was forced to break into the discussions every two or three minutes as the discussion over limited prohibition of drink grew animated.[11] It would not be surprising if he wished for some more congenial and peaceable colleagues to work with. On Tuesday 20 April 1915 Asquith travelled to Newcastle to deliver a speech, which many commentators have viewed as the biggest blunder of his ministry. It was not.

He told 5,000 munition workers that there was not a word of truth that the operations of the army were being hampered by the failure of the government to provide the necessary ammunition. The reason he did so was because Sir John French had told Kitchener this, and Kitchener had said it to Asquith. With such a weight of assurance, Asquith simply gave the information that he had; if he could not believe such sources, then whom could he believe? Surely it is reasonable for a Prime Minister to believe what he is told by the Secretary for War and the Commander in Chief of his army in the field.

French had given the assurance to Kitchener on 14 April that he had all the ammunition that his troops would be able to use on the next forward movement. It is true that there were letters arriving from France that spoke of shortages of ammunition; Viscount Sandhurst, the Lord Chamberlain, spoke of receiving such on 7 April, so at least one Liberal intimate of Asquith, who had appointed him to his post in 1912, was aware of the situation, at least in hearsay. However, the Commander in Chief of the BEF had assured the Prime Minister that he had all the ammunition he needed. Thus, the Prime Minister gave what was designed to be a morale boosting speech to vital war workers and told them the truth that he knew; the version from the highest authorities, the men he had placed in charge, rather than listening to gossip. French even wrote to Kitchener again on 2 May:

'The ammunition will be all right.'[12]

He told Kitchener[13] that the artillery bombardment at Neuve Chappelle had been the minimum necessary, although he had been stressing the need for more munitions for weeks whenever he was interviewed. The real reason for his dissembling was not to become apparent until much later. Lloyd George lifted the curtain of secrecy somewhat as to numbers in a speech in the Commons on 22 April in which he said that the government had organized for war at the start, with six divisions and now had 36, that is to say 720,000 men actually at the front. He also said that production had switched from mainly shrapnel to mainly high explosive shells, and that the expenditure of ammunition had far exceeded the estimate of all the armies.[14] Deep in a power struggle with Kitchener for control of ammunition supply at this time, Lloyd George saw no problems at all in telling the editor of the *News of the World* on 24 April that there was a shortage of ammunition, despite Kitchener and French's assurances that there was not and despite the impression that his speech gave the Commons.[15]

Asquith told the King on 8 April[16] that approaches were made to Lansdowne and Bonar Law to postpone voter registration and an election for a year and to enter into discussion with the opposition leaders on that subject. The last election had been in December 1910 and the mandate of the government would run out in December 1915. The only conceivable offer that he could possibly make the Conservatives in order for them to agree to extend the life of Parliament, was to have some sort of say in government. In other words, coalition was inevitable, for if it did not come then there would have to be an election, in wartime, with hundreds of thousands of electors fighting abroad. Bonar Law was not happy, as he wrote to Lansdowne on 13 April:

'The proposal of the government, as usual is intended to get the utmost possible advantage out of the situation. Their proposal, as it stands, would mean that they would have a perfectly free hand to have an election any time between now and the end of the 6 years ... I am inclined to think that our best course is to decline any arrangement just now... if it is inevitable that an election this year cannot be held without disadvantage to the country we should be prepared to consider reasonable proposals ... we ought to keep a free hand as long as possible...(Asquith's proposals)

1 As emergency measure, present Parliament authorized to continue for 6 years instead of 5.

2 For purposes of Parliament act, next session to be treated as continuation of this session'.[17]

In keeping a free hand, it is clear that Bonar Law wished to keep his options open as regarded an election, for as long as possible. Lansdowne penciled at the bottom of this letter:

'Why not session to last till end of war and truce?'

Clearly Lansdowne saw some sort of accommodation as inevitable and desirable.

Asquith must have known that there was no way that the Conservatives would accept a prolongation of Parliament beyond the end of the year unless they had a say in government. If this was an offer at coalition, Asquith lost nothing - he had been Prime Minister of an elected government since December 1910. His mandate was due to expire in somewhat under seven months. Something had to give. If he was not prepared to concede a say in government, then there is no reason why Lansdowne should have even considered a longer arrangement; after all, if making an arrangement was delayed until December then his party would be in a much stronger position from which to dictate terms.

Some form of accommodation was on offer from Asquith to Bonar Law in mid April, as the price for extending the life of the Parliament, but the Conservative leader did not act on it. That he did act in May indicates that additional pressure came from elsewhere that made him act. Certainly there was pressure from some of the Press, as Margot Asquith indicated on 21 April:

'The Times editor, a real blackguard of the lowest kind, has openly boasted he will do for Henry.   He wants a Coalition Gov- LlG Prime Minister, Austen Home Office, B Law Foreign Office (or vice versa) H Ld Chancellor etc...' [18]

She obviously had taken against Geoffrey Robinson, but if he wanted a coalition then it was even more indicative of a great divide among the Conservatives between those who did, and those who did not.

Finally, the main pressure to go into coalition must have been on Bonar Law for the simple reason that he could not wait until December and a possible election. By that time it was very likely that he would no longer have been leading his party and for two very strong reasons involving compulsion, and a shipment of ore. He *had* to do something.

Compulsion in the Air

On the question of compulsion, Asquith had to bear in mind the temper of those who might be compelled. The mood of the eighty percent of British people who comprised the working class, had been increasingly militant in 1914, and the unionisation of society was proceeding quickly from 2.5 millions in 1914 to 8.5 millions in 1918. Something approaching a general strike had been planned for October 1914 in mines, transport and railways unions, and had been averted by the outbreak of war. If national unity was to be maintained then the concerns of Labour had to be listened to. Vernon Hartshorn, leader of the notoriously militant South Wales miners visited George Riddell on 23 April and told him that Robert Smillie, President of the Mineworkers Union had been to see Asquith with other miners' leaders.[19] Smillie made a speech, which explained that although his members were prepared to sacrifice themselves in the national interest, they were not prepared to do so in the interests of the masters who were making enormous profits. Hartshorn thought Asquith was frightened at the prospect of another coal strike, but if that is so, then his fear did not show when he wrote to Venetia about the meeting. The Prime Minister mollified them, arranged to meet the coal owners with them and thought it possible to 'put the screw on both'.[20] Asquith was evidently aware that, even though he did not have to maintain good press relations, he had to maintain good labour relations. Arthur Henderson, the Labour leader was supporting the government, but he hinted that he could withdraw support – his party was still angry about Lloyd George and drink, whilst some workers at Woolwich building houses for munition workers were threatening to go on strike for a war bonus. London County Council (LCC) tram workers were about to bring London's trams to a halt for 3 days over pay; Labour and labour had to be kept onside and as happy as possible. Any attempt to compel the working man into the army at this time would be resisted.

On 21 April the Conservative back bench spoke out in the House, in the person of Professor Hewins, Long's number two at the Unionist Business Committee, who took over its leadership the following year. He was also a close personal friend of Long. Hewins stressed that what had been achieved after nine months of war was marvelous, but that he thought a lot more could be done, that some of what was done now should have been done before, and that better organization was needed, particularly in the supply of munitions. He did not think drink impaired industrial efficiency, thus setting on record his disagreement, and hence that of others too, with his party leader. In the course of his speech he stated that he was not prejudiced, but he was against teetotalism. Bonar Law was, of course a teetotaler. Hewins was not a major figure in the party, though eminent in the field of economics, and his remarks were prefixed with the statement that he did not wish to criticize the government - he was advising them. For a back bench MP to say something like this was a bold step, but not so very bold if he was speaking as a mouthpiece for someone of more weight.

Sir Basil Peto, in rising to second what Hewins had said, reinforced much of what had been said, but went further, a lot further:

' ...*it seems to me that the Government, realizing the importance of the tremendous problem that we are up against, should at the very outset have organized a national war service. They should have recognized, as the Prime Minister made so clear in his speech yesterday, that men engaged in the shipyards, men engaged even in the coal mines underground, and certainly men engaged in the engineering trades, were working and doing a part of absolutely the same national job as the men engaged in fighting in Flanders at the front. It rested with the Government to lay down the conditions under which every man in the country could best serve the State and, if they had made it clear to the people of the country at the outset, I am quite sure, whatever rules they had found it necessary to make, and whatever powers they had found it necessary to take, would not only have been met and accepted without resentment, but would have been met and accepted gladly and willingly, and it would have given a sense of security to the country as a whole. They could have made their own rules, and they could have taken measures to see that those rules were observed... They should establish a national war service for all military and civil employment.*' [21]*

Thus the question of compulsory national service, which the Conservative leaders had not wished to be brought up, was finally ventilated in the House of Commons, but not by Long. Peto was the Conservative MP for Devizes in Wiltshire, and a close neighbour and associate in that country of Walter Long, who had formerly been MP for Devizes and whose house and 4,100-acre estate was at Rood Ashton, Wiltshire.

In 1988 Keith Grieves followed Beaverbrook and identified Walter Long as the foremost Unionist advocate of Compulsory Service and stated that it was he that marshaled opposition to the continuation of voluntaryism and it is not hard to see his hand behind this demand for national service.[22]

Mr George Roberts of Labour, who had not contemplated speaking in the debate did so, because he found Sir Basil's remarks to be tactless. He was much incensed, but he did tone down his comments:

' ...I think it extremely undesirable that unnecessary divisions should be aroused during this great national emergency.' [23]

Bonar Law then made a long speech in which he also criticized the government's lack of organization and the alleged shortage of ammunition at the front, but of national service or compulsion he said not a word. He did say this however:

I am getting constantly criticized by my own friends, in letters, because we do not criticize the Government enough. Where are we to draw the line? My experience in this House is that you cannot have sham fights. Once you begin, it is very difficult to draw the line.[24]

He might have avoided it studiously, but it did not stop his back benchers, or the newspapers from talking about it the Conservative member for Devonport, Sir Clement Kinloch-Cooke, asked Mr Tennant, Under Secretary of war about it on 4 May:

'*Sir C. KINLOCH-COOKE asked the Under-Secretary of State for War whether his attention has been called to statements made at Hull by Major-General Bowles, C.B., War Office Inspector of Recruiting, to the effect that in going about the country he has heard suggestions as to compulsory service; that he had reported these suggestions to the War Office and been told not to make any further refer-once to compulsion; will he say whether the statements are made with the knowledge and consent of the Secretary of State for War; and, if not, on whose authority?*

Mr TENNANT I am informed that Major-General Bowles, C.B., stated that, though he had heard suggestions as to compulsory service when going about the country, it would save the time of the meeting if the attention of those present were confined to the question of obtaining recruits under existing conditions. He added that the War Office was not then considering the question of compulsion, and that reference, therefore, need not be made to the subject during the discussion. Major-General Bowles' duties are to assist in raising recruits, and he has no concern with questions of recruiting policy.

Sir C. KINLOCH-COOKE *Is the right hon. Gentleman aware that the statements about which I have put this question have appeared in almost every paper throughout the country; and can he say whether all those reports are wrong?* [25]

Mr Tennant dismissed this last by stating that what he had said was accurate, but the issue of Compulsion was clearly not going away. Lord Beaverbrook, years later, said that Bonar Law 'quelled' the activities of the UBC, maintaining his position of patriotic opposition and objecting to the UBC's continued drawing of attention to the shortage of ammunition. During the latter part of April and the early part of May the pressure from the Conservative backbench for compulsion was growing until eventually it reached uncontrollable proportions by mid May.

On 22 April, HA Gwynne, whom Asquith considered to be the maniac who edited the *Morning Post*, wrote at length to the Prime Minister with a long list of advice on what he should be doing. Towards the end of his essay he wrote that whilst he was an ardent supporter of compulsory service, he had not, so far, pushed it during this war, but he had to say that he felt that without some form of national service, then Britain would be at a disadvantage at a future peace conference.[26] He did not specify why this might be so, but it was clear that the question of compulsion was, by this time, very high on some Conservative's wish lists. By the first half of May it was to be higher still.

A Shortage of Shells

Beaverbrook had Lloyd George as being the man who inspired Northcliffe to take up the ammunition shortage in his newspapers.[27] Following Peter Fraser's 1982 exposure of Beaverbrook's fabrications,[28] what he said must be treated with care, but it is certain that Northcliffe did act.

On 1 May 1915 Lord Northcliffe wrote a letter to Sir John French, Commander of the British Expeditionary Force (BEF) in France, that was to spark off what became known as the Shell Scandal. Northcliffe's letter still makes alarming reading. He told French that Lloyd George had stated in the House of Commons that French had an army of 35 divisions:

'...If Sir John French has 750 000 men, why is he only holding 30 miles of line?...you are therefore believed to have this vast army at your disposal... in the absence of some strong statement from you the government have your friends at their mercy because they are able to say that any agitation is unpatriotic and playing the enemy's game. As a further result of secrecy Mr Asquith is able to assure the nation that your operations have never been hampered for want of ammunition... the inevitable result of secrecy will be to cast blame upon you ... A short and very vigorous statement from you to a private correspondent... would, I believe, render the government's position impossible...'[29]

Northcliffe's portrayal of an underhand Asquith misinforming Parliament in an attempt to shift the blame for slow progress in the war onto French is about as far from most descriptions of Asquith as may be read. In fact he was notorious for his loyalty in backing up the people he had appointed. It was a clear attempt to stampede French, and it succeeded probably beyond Northcliffe's wildest dreams. The press baron may have been given a clear insight into the character of the man he was dealing with by someone quite close to him, and thus a good idea of how he would react. *The Times* on 4 May stated that there was a want of ammunition at the front, which prompted the Lord Chamberlain to ask Balfour if what Asquith had said at Newcastle was true. Balfour replied that of course it was true, but what was really wanted was a supply for a month ahead, which we did not have, but would get.[30] So there was no shortage of ammunition, but of a reserve of ammunition.

French did give a vigorous statement, to Charles A'Court Repington, the war correspondent of *The Times,* Northcliffe's man who was a personal friend of the General of many year's standing. Any mystery as to why French took this action, a man who had protested to Asquith and to Kitchener not long before that he had all the ammunition he needed and could not hope for a better Prime Minister behind him, may be cleared up by imagining the General's utter panic at the thought of being made the scapegoat for his staff's failings. Doubtless Repington would have magnified this in conversation. Repington was a rather louche character who had been forced to resign from the army over an 'affair of honour'. Well known for his right-wing views and militaristic outlook, he was popularly known among Liberals as 'Wreckington'. He was also present at French's headquarters without consultation between French and Kitchener, which Kitchener did not like.

It is possible that Repington himself had prompted Northcliffe to write to French, because French had remarked to him that the failure of the British attack on Neuve Chappelle in March 1915 had been due to lack of artillery ammunition. We must presume that French did not mention either the fact that he had been instructed earlier in the year not to make any forward movements until the supply of ammunition had improved,[31] or that he had assured the Prime Minister that he had plenty of ammunition. He may have also omitted the piece of information that despite his instructions, the British army had fired more ammunition during the Neuve Chappelle battle than in the whole of the South African War. Perhaps somewhere in this may be seen the bare fact that to demand an unlimited supply of ammunition at this date was completely unrealistic. Factories, raw, materials, skilled labour and the infrastructure that supports them just do not appear as if by magic; before 1914 the British arms industry was miniscule by continental standards simply because the British army was tiny.

French had panicked previously during the retreat to the Marne in 1914 when he had sent the Cabinet via Kitchener a message declaring his intention to take his army out of the fighting line:

' I shall absolutely be unable to remain in the front line as he (the French commander) has now begun his retirement. I have decided to begin my retirement tomorrow, in the morning, behind the Seine in a south westerly direction, west of Paris. This means marching for some 8 days without fatiguing the troops, at a considerable distance from the enemy. It will be possible for us to commence our reorganization on the road. My base is now in the neighbourhood of La Rochelle.'[32]

This strange proposition to march his troops, without tiring them, on a walking tour right across France to a place from where they would probably be evacuated had been the occasion when Kitchener was hurriedly dispatched to France to strengthen French's backbone. The BEF Commander took umbrage from the Secretary of State's being in uniform, implying that he outranked French; which he certainly did anyway. He was to panic again before the end of 1915, advocating a negotiated peace after failing to break through after massive casualties at the Battle of Loos in September. Suspicious and choleric by nature, French's knee-jerk reaction to Northcliffe's threat, for such it was, is not surprising; above all it gives substance to Northcliffe's later boasts that he had brought down the Liberal government. Subsequently this led to the press baron's assertion that he brought down the coalition in December 1916 and to his threatening to bring down Lloyd George if the then Prime Minister did not include him in the post war government.

French actually had nothing to fear. Asquith had made a rare intervention in military strategy on 9 January 1915 when he sent French a note in which he explained to him that he must not attack on the western front, but must hold the line he had; efforts were being made all over the world, as far away as Japan to secure ammunition but the supply could not sustain an attack at this time. French's brief was thus quite clear for the early part of 1915; on 14 April 1915 he had a discussion with Kitchener who later wrote to Asquith:

'I have had a talk with French. He told me that with the present supply of ammunition he will have as much as his troops will be able to use on the next forward movement'.[33]

French may well have had another and much simpler reason for his statement. He had mounted a large attack because he had received a large reinforcement of troops that had more than replaced the casualties of 1914; the Indians and Canadians had arrived with their equipment and it may have seemed that spring was the right time for a break through on the western front, and it nearly succeeded because of the gallantry of those involved. However, the battle of Neuve Chappelle was a bungled affair, but not because of the shortage of ammunition. There had been a breakdown of logistics and the supporting artillery had not been moved into its proper places after the first initial success. Fully five hours elapsed between the first and second attacks, allowing the Germans time to regroup, dig new positions and move from old ones. At least half of the troops who attacked did so without supporting artillery on unbombarded positions, and, as a result, their attack failed; and this is not surprising given the failings in the plan of attack. Huge amounts of ammunition had been fired at places where there was no enemy. Worse, as Hew Strachan pointed out, when eventually the British artillery re-opened fire at 3.30pm on 10 March, they were zeroed in on the wrong targets and hit their own infantry.[34]

Although Douglas Haig, the Field Commander had made extensive use of aerial photographs in his planning, the interpretation of such images was in its infancy. A formidable line of German obstacles had been missed and were not included in the artillery firing schedules at all. If they had possessed double the ammunition their efforts would still have been in vain. This is all entirely besides the fact that Haig's Corps commanders failed to carry out their orders and threw away what was a perfectly feasible plan of attack if it had been carried out properly. It was so much easier to blame failure on a shortage of ammunition. As Brigadier General CR Ballard later commented:

'The final results (at Neuve Chappelle) were not glorious. The excuse found was lack of shells, and particularly of High Explosive shells. Henceforward it became the excuse for everything.[35]

Ballard thought that blaming a shortage of ammunition on failures to break through the German lines was absurd, pointing to attacks where the French fired over 1,000 rounds a minute at German positions and still failed to break them. He was a very experienced and well-placed officer whose comments on the matter may not be dismissed lightly. His view was that the war had produced conditions which no-one had expected and that no-one involved in the command of the Neuve Chappelle battle had any conceivable right to throw stones at Kitchener for shortage of high explosives. He also pointed out that the 1,200,000 HE shells that were delivered in October 1915, for which Lloyd George got the credit as Minister of Munitions, were all ordered before May 1915, by Kitchener.

During May 1915 over 400 field pieces fired over 100,000 rounds during the battle of Festubert but the Germans had effective defences and the heavy rain that started during the attack also led to failure. Sir John French would perhaps have done better to look at his own staff and planning before claiming that shortage of ammunition led to the failure; but mendacity has uses in politics and some politicians make excellent scapegoats.

There was no 'shortage' of ammunition to any reasonable person after nine months of war; not only was this pointed out by Asquith, but Kitchener who, as the war went on, got more canny with the press and planted a small piece of information with George Riddell, editor of the *News of the World*, on 27 May 1915 after being accused of keeping the army short of ammunition:

'...such lies, such damned lies..have been circulated. Under ordinary circumstances I should take measures, but in the face of the Germans what can I do? French has plenty of ammunition at Havre. Why does he leave it there? Here are the figures..'[36]

Kitchener revealed his distress to Riddell at what he saw as Sir John French's 'breach of discipline' and spelled out how much ammunition he was actually sending him. Here is an indication again that the problem was the army's own systems of logistics, yet it was French, panicking, who precipitated the so called shell scandal by leaking the information to *The Times* that there was a shortage - perhaps what the Tories and Northcliffe most wished to hear and contrary to what French had told Kitchener. Certainly it diverted any possible attention away from the actual battles themselves and the planning of them. It is little wonder that John Burns wrote in his diary on 3 May 1915:

'...the Northcliffe gang like wolves, are hanging onto the government sleigh.' [37]

Kitchener, much excoriated for his 'secrecy' and reluctance to divulge what he was doing to his Cabinet colleagues, had in fact much reason to be wary of the Press. He did brief the press himself however, speaking to George Riddell on numerous occasions, but wished to retain control over what was said. The government also, in placing stringent restrictions on press activities in France, was fully justified, considering the actions of the Northcliffe Press at the opening of the war as the editor of the *Manchester Guardian* CP Scott wrote to Leonard Hobhouse on 26 September 1914:

'Last night there came an instruction from the Press Bureau so stringent that it will almost prevent any sort of comment on the War. It is the result of the Times and the Daily Mail giving away the flanking movement of the allies. They actually stated which of the French divisions had been moved to the left flank- most important information for the Germans....' [38]

With actions such as this in many countries, the offending newspapers would have been closed down and the editors imprisoned. Northcliffe was left alone, though increasingly resentful at what he saw as undue censorship during the winter of 1914-15. Eventually, like Trollope's Tom Towers of the *Jupiter*, he exhibited delusions of grandeur perhaps seeing himself as the arbiter of mighty forces, writing to HG Wells on 8 May:

'It is only when one looks at the world through the microscope of a newspaper that one sees how reputations are made ...the wrong men often rise to the surface.'

Having labeled the government as the 'wrong men' he then revealed himself to be plainly among the advocates of authoritarianism, and thus an enemy of Democracy, at least the Liberal kind:

'...we are now heading towards a food shortage. One strong man who would order the people to eat less would effect the desired result. The reason I support (Edward Carson) is because he is really anxious about the war and as far as I can learn the only other prominent politician anxious about the war is Mr Lloyd George [39]

Asquith, Grey, Haldane et al, we must presume, were not anxious about the war; they should have consulted Northcliffe on how to conduct it. Or more moderately, JL Garvin, who wrote a lead article in *The Observer* on 9 May. He did not attack the government or the Prime Minister - he was in a way quite flattering. Although he trusted them all, and stated that any group of men would have made mistakes in the running of the war, he did feel that perhaps now there should be 'an all party committee of public safety'. He wanted a cross party approach to the war and nor was he alone. Balfour gave a speech on 10 May which included the sentence:

'I should like to see, in the conduct of our righteous cause, something of that unity of purpose and fixity of action which has characterized our German enemies in all their wretchedness. [40]

Calls for unity seemed to be coming from all angles.

Bonar Law on the Edge

On 6 May Lloyd George introduced his budget into the House and proposed heavily increased taxation on drink; in view of Bonar Law's previous support of his notions of controlling drink, he might have been puzzled when Bonar Law came out against him and thought the taxes too heavy. In fact he was not against taxes of themselves, but was attempting to calm down his own back-bench, and especially the UBC who wished to challenge the government on the subject, and to whom their leader's compromise was not acceptable. His miscalculation had backfired on him very badly and the drinks trade was up in arms against Lloyd George's proposals. Indignant deputations were visiting Bonar Law from the drinks industry and making their feelings very plain. Newspapers both national and regional thundered against the threat to ruin a great industry whilst Irish brewers and farmers held a resentful meeting in Phoenix Park to protest. Bonar Law had actually sent a note to Professor Hewins that he and his friends should take no part in the debate; somehow he needed to repair his position. Hewins sent a reply and noted indignantly in his diary:

'...to which I replied we were competent to form our own judgment on the position'.[41]

The Conservative backbench was on the point of revolt and Bonar Law could not direct his own men. Bonar Law was very vulnerable at this time as his family firm, Jacks & Co, was about to be put on trial for trading with the enemy; his elder brother John (Jack) Law was to appear for the prosecution. On 6 May 1915 a letter appeared in the Socialist magazine *Justice* written by the veteran leader of the Social Democratic Federation (SDF) Henry Hyndman. It included the following paragraph:

'Undoubtedly our government is weak, incompetent, tyrannous and Germanophil. A cabal of the old Charle II sort. But its policy is, practically, backed up by the Opposition. No wonder if it is true, that Mr Bonar Law's own firm has been 'trading with the enemy', and his own brother is out on heavy bail for that alleged offence.'[42]

Having read this, Bonar Law drafted a speech of resignation which is preserved in his papers. It includes this about his brother:

'...if it should be proved that he has been guilty I should not be willing to continue in Public Life and I should at once resign the position that I now hold.[43]

If this was a major factor in deciding Bonar Law's actions in mid May, it might go a long way towards explaining why he was prepared to take the comparatively lowly office of Colonial Secretary in the upcoming coalition, providing, as it did, a shelter from his own right-wing. It is worthwhile considering the mentality of the situation. A man of 58, much travelled, experienced in business and in life, accustomed to operating at the highest levels in the land sat down and wrote a resignation speech. This is not something that is normal or everyday It takes time and thought and is a measure of last resort - a voluntary falling onto a metaphorical and political sword. It is also very revealing of a troubled mind. If the SS Themis was not steaming at something less than 8.5 knots through Bonar Law's troubled brain in the wee hours of the morning then he would be something more than human. It is not the speech of a man in a strong position. This is the speech of a man in trouble, seeing it, and being forced to the realisation that he might have to go, and it does not matter that the speech was never delivered; the speech was written, and that is enough to include it as a factor in the formation of the 1915 coalition - and perhaps a major one.

His resignation speech, moreover, does not hold water; he stated that he had ceased his connection with the company in 1901, but gave it up absolutely when he entered Parliament:

' I have from time to time put money on deposit with them at a fixed rate of interest, I have had no share, direct or indirect with the profits or losses of the firm...During the 13 years the amount has varied, entirely to suit my convenience, between what was for me considerable sums and a few hundred pounds... This connection, so for as I can see is precisely the same and involves no other responsibility than that of everyone with his bankers.' [44]

On the back of his speech draft he wrote how much he had on deposit at Jacks & Co; remember these are the values of 1914 and that various authorities reckon the 1914 figure may be multiplied between 60 and 95 times to understand its modern purchasing power.

1903	£9,500
1904	£770
1905	£3,145
1906	£7,491
1907	£590
1908	£9,137
1909	£7,132
1910	£9,226
1911	£4,817
1912	£14,352
1913	£13,758
1914	£6,525

So for most of the time between 1903 and 1914, despite his deprecation of it, Bonar Law had on deposit at interest in Jacks & Co what amounted to a King's ransom to the man in the street.

Until Hyndman's letter appeared in *Justice* the whole Jacks affair had not entered the public domain in that there had been no coverage of it in the newspapers. The letter makes it obvious that it was 'out there' in the sense that some people knew of it and it was being talked about, but as far as the press was concerned the blackout appears to have been total. In part this may be because the Conservative dominated media would not wish to hurt their own leader, but it does not entirely explain the silence of the Liberal press. This perhaps indicates that press censorship was responsible in suppressing something which might reasonably be used by the enemy in their propaganda; or an unwillingness by Liberals to bring it into public notice. Whatever the reason, when it became clear that Jack Law was not to be prosecuted and the trial commenced in June, it received the widest possible press coverage, with some reporters' accounts being almost verbatim of witness statements. To Bonar Law on 6 May the Hyndman letter must have appeared as the first trickle of a dyke about to burst. HA Taylor, in his 1932 biography of Bonar Law stated that by May it still was not clear that Jack Law would not be prosecuted; his brother was right to be anxious.

It is to be hoped that a certain sense of sheepishness lay behind what moved him to preserve an article from *Justice* which appeared in July 1915:

' *It is much to be regretted that the House of Commons...should be so subject to fits of indecent hypocrisy. Anybody would imagine, at such times, that wholesale profiteering was not the daily preoccupation of its members. Never was there a worse case of this habitual hypocrisy than Mr Bonar Law's connection with the house of Messrs Jacks & Co. Mr Law was a member of this firm until 1901. Then he withdrew from any active participation in the business or share in the total profits. That is all right and honourable. Nobody supposes for a moment that he personally had anything to do with the disreputable 'trading with the enemy' which has just got Messrs Jacks & Co, including Mr Law's brother, into serious trouble. But, as Mr Law himself admits, he had left an important capital sum, at a fixed rate of interest, in his old firm. Whence is the interest on this money derived? Obviously, from the profits obtained by trading with Mr Bonar Law's money, originally accumulated itself from the surplus value of the business... Mr Law is no martyr at all...* ' [45]

That is exactly so. Whatever Bonar Law said, a close scrutiny of what he had said would reveal that even at fixed interest, he had shared the profits of Jacks & Co and so, by association, had profited if they profited, and had had derived that profit from where they derived it - some from Germany.

If Bonar law's family firm had been trading with the enemy, then such was the mood of the time that he could not possibly survive it. Prince Louis of Battenberg had resigned the previous year over his German origins. RB Haldane, the architect of the British Army, was being pilloried in the right wing press as being pro-German, but the atmosphere of public life in May 1915 was fetid with hatred and fear of the Germans. Zeppelins had bombed the London docks on 12 February, but no raids on London itself had yet taken place. Ipswich was attacked on 29-30 April, and Southend on 9-10 May. The first raid on London itself was not until 31 May. Nonetheless, feelings against Germans were running at fever pitch. Anti-German rioting had broken out in the East End of London, and it was reported in the *Leamington Spa Courier* on 7 May that 30 cases of riotous behaviour had been tried by the Thames Police Court the previous day. In the first week of May there are few mentions of riots recorded in newspapers; by the second week the regional newspapers were full of widespread riots as anti-German hysteria escalated out of control. The news of the sinking of the Lusitania on 8 May sparked violent demonstrations and riots as German owned shops and businesses were demolished in several towns. A perfect storm of blind fury targeted anything that even remotely looked German.

At Doncaster a shop belonging to an Englishman was attacked by a mob of 2,000 miners in mistake for a German business, and he fired a gun into the crowd to scare them off.[46] The police made several baton charges against the mob then arrested the proprietor, a Mr Bakewell, supposed to be a German, for firing his gun. In the East End of London there was widespread looting of shops, hairdressers and premises of all kinds, goods of all sorts being carried off in wheelbarrows. In Liverpool, reputedly 50 'German' shops were looted and set on fire. A rally of thousands of 'city men' on Tower Hill demanded the rounding up and deportation of all Germans whilst anyone connected with Germany in any way was hustled violently out of the stock exchange and the Baltic exchange. The riots spread throughout the land with reports from places such as Salford, Doncaster, Rotherham and Sheffield as well as many other towns and cities.[47] A rumour that the battleship HMS Queen Elizabeth had been sunk at the Dardanelles on 12 May, added to the monstrous anger of the mobs. In fact she had not – it was HMS Goliath, a pre Dreadnought that had been sunk, after which the Queen Elizabeth moved to a safer location. Wild rumours circulated the country, one of them being of a mysterious sailor in New York who had prophesied that London would be in flames within a month.   That the Southend Zeppelin bombing had killed an old woman caused especial outrage.[48]

On 10 May an outbreak of anti-German rioting and looting took pace in Bootle, Bonar Law's own constituency, and must have focused his mind on what to do about the large numbers of 'aliens' living in Britain who were the epicentre of the widespread disturbances.   It did not matter what nationality they were - Russians, Swiss, Italians - anyone foreign was being attacked and their premises looted.   Asquith set out measures in Parliament on 12 May to deal with registration and internment of aliens, which would satisfy public demand for him to do so, and Bonar Law replied in strong support of his proposals. He then went on;

From the first, throughout this War, I have very much disliked, and I have persistently avoided, taking any share of responsibility for the action of a Government over which I could have no possible control; but I thought the question in regard to these outbreaks so serious, from the point of view of the national credit, if nothing else, that I took the liberty of discussing the matter with the Prime Minister yesterday. After hearing the course which the Government proposed to adopt, and which the right hon. Gentleman has outlined to-day, I said to him—and I think it right to say it publicly— that I could think of no better plan than that which is now proposed to the House of Commons.[49]

Cooperation, cordial discussion and agreement had clearly become a normal thing between Bonar Law and Asquith, whether a coalition was in prospect or not.   The next stage would be logical and not too much of a leap.

On 13 May the heavy rioting continued in E and SE London and troops had to be called out whilst Asquith announced that enemy aliens were to be arrested and interned, whilst 40,000 naturalised Germans were to have their cases investigated by the Home Office.   Some sort of control was re-established in the riot areas by 14 May, but sporadic outbreaks continued for some days, notably at Walton on Thames on 17 May.[50]

In this miasma of febrile and hysterical hostility to anything German, any suggestion that Bonar Law was involved in any way would and should have been the end of him.   Reason had flown out of the window.   To cap it all, it was not just any commodity that Jacks & Co had supplied to the enemy, but iron ore - the very stuff to make the guns and bullets that were killing the British soldiers whose derring-do, gallantry, and deaths were making headlines daily in every newspaper, let alone torpedoes that sank British Cunarders and battleships, and Zeppelin bombs that killed old ladies.

Bonar Law had also realised that he did not have the wholehearted support of his party either, and the teetotaller who had told Lloyd George that the Conservative party would not oppose his measures to control drink in April, at the beginning of May told him that the Conservatives could not approve the size of the raised taxes he proposed to levy in his budget, scheduled to be introduced on 4 May.[51]

In the debate Bonar Law was equivocal:

'I am sure there is an evil, and that to some extent—how great I do not know—that evil is aggravated by the system under which drink is obtained in those areas. That is an evil which we are bound to do our best to remedy, but the remedy must not be out of proportion to the evil.[52]

Opposition to controls on drink within his party had forced him to revise his position- and had quite clearly annoyed some within the Conservative Party. Bonar Law continued:

'I am absolutely convinced that if those taxes are proceeded with on anything like the present basis you will have throughout the length and breadth of England an agitation precisely of the same kind as we had in regard to the Licensing Bill of 1908. I have every evidence of it now, for since I have been sitting here I do not know how many telegrams I have received, and I have been inundated with deputations...[53]

It must have been somewhat embarrassing to be in the position of having said the Conservatives would not oppose buying out and controlling the drinks industry, and regretting the ties between his party and drink, then having to perform a U-turn against the compromise with which Lloyd George had ended up. Bonar Law was not in charge of his party any more and the tail was wagging the dog.

If the opposition wanted Bonar Law's scalp, then this was the time to have it; he had one foot in his political coffin and the other on a bar of soap. By no stretch of the imagination was this man personally or politically in a position of strength; and yet the Conservative leader, who was on the ropes if any politician ever was, who had his resignation speech ready, and who faced the disgrace of his family and business, is supposed

110

to have forced a government with a majority in the House to resign one week later; a government whose leader knew about the Jacks case and had done for months.

That beggars belief.

Bonar Law was in dire trouble, and, as John Stubbs said in 1975, he saw that the only way to rescue his position was to move his party towards a 'proffered coalition'- this had been proffered for some time in fact, and now he needed it:

'...Not to have done so would have destroyed his credibility as leader. This was one of the lessons learned from the partisan struggle over drink. The May crisis provided a clear illustration of the changing relationship, generated by the politics of war, between the Unionist leadership and its parliamentary supporters. To see the Unionist Parliamentary party as a docile and deferential group of well-drilled back-benchers working in close harmony with their leaders is most misleading.[54]

He did not even have to figure it out for himself- his own Chief Whip, Arthur Steel-Maitland revealed later:

'I may have been responsible in some small measure for the Coalition as for some weeks past I have been pressing on Bonar Law the fact that it was probably the best solution to the present difficulty, and that he would soon have to face a decision with regard to it.' [55]

Thus, in mid May 1915 it was not so much Asquith in trouble politically, but Bonar Law who was now driven to do things he would not otherwise have done.

Chapter 7

Mr Long Gives Some Advice

As well as the potential ruin of his good name and that of his brother and his family firm, Bonar Law was facing rebellion in his own party on three counts, only the drinks issue being of his own making. That many of the backbench wanted active opposition was the second issue, but compulsion, so urgent to Walter Long and his followers was about to become the focus round which he could marshal the strength to pacify his party, his own problem being that he did not like the idea. Before the publication of Repington's article about shells, and before the impending resignation of Fisher, Long wrote to Bonar Law on 12 May:

'I am writing to say that it looks to me as if pressure for a national government might be irresistible - & I only want to say that I hope you won't worry about whom you take with you. I would gladly 'stand down'. Whatever you do, you will have us all solid behind you.' [1]

This seeming self-effacement was hugely at odds with what he wrote 4 days later when he was solid against coalition. Certainly, on 13 May a coalition was not in prospect:

*'51. **Mr. BOOTH** asked the Prime Minister whether, in view of the present War and in view of the steps necessary to be taken in order to grapple with the rearrangement of industry and social life consequent upon a prolonged struggle, he will consider the desirability of admitting into the ranks of Ministers leading Members of the various political parties in this House?*

The PRIME MINISTER *The Government are greatly indebted to the leading Members of all parties for suggestions and assistance of certain specific subjects. The step suggested by my hon. Friend is not in contemplation, and I am not aware that it would meet with general assent'.* [2]

It is curious that Asquith was asked this question by a long serving Liberal MP, but it gave him a chance to express his indebtedness to contributions made by the opposition, that he was open to suggestions and assistance from them, but also that he did not think it would be supported. The bulk of Liberal MPs certainly did not want a coalition, as they were later to make clear to Asquith, so the statement must also have reassured them. However, it was quite correct that a coalition was not in contemplation because it did not lie in Asquith's power to form one; he could only do that if the opposition were willing to take part. John Burns noted in his diary on 13 May:

'Just now rumours of coalition, resented by Liberals not led by opposition but being pushed by Northcliffe who really believes that he should run which views run the country'.[3]

These rumours were being fed, in part, by Churchill, who had never disguised his wish to see a coalition; a wish not shared by Margot who wrote on 3 May:

' Winston is always gassing about a coalition Gov. - so disloyal to his PM. I should loathe a coalition, so would H...' [4]

It would be a mistake to think that Margot knew Asquith's mind, for there was so much about him that remained enigma to her, but her prescience at times was notable. On 13 May she further remarked:

'What a satire if the coming coalition govt of which Winston has gassed so much, should not contain him! I know H too well to suppose this, but there is no doubt that if Henry wanted to make himself supremely popular with every party, ours and the others, he would exclude Winston...'[5]

Nor was Churchill the only Liberal Minister in favour of a coalition. Lloyd George had suggested one to sort out the nation's problems back in August 1910 in a long memorandum which he was shortly to re-circulate:

'The equality of the parties in number is, in itself, a source of weakness for it means that Government has only to alienate a comparatively small number of the Electorate in order to incur defeat, and an Opposition has only to win the support of the same number in order to oust their opponents from power.'

Thus, often the least responsible, the least well informed and the most selfish among the Electorate may have a decisive voice in determining the issues upon which the future of the whole British Empire may depend.

If joint action between the Parties could be negotiated, these undesirable elements would sink to their proper insignificance as factors.'[6]

Quite clearly there was no need to convince the Chancellor of the Exchequer of the virtues of Coalition to face problems best solved jointly.

Repington's article accusing the government of not supplying enough ammunition to the army was published in *The Times* and *The Daily Mail* on 14 May. It contradicted what Asquith had said to munition workers at Newcastle and gave a clear inference that he had been deceiving the nation as to the actual supply of ammunition. It did not meet with popular approval in its criticisms of Kitchener; copies of both newspapers were burned on the Stock Exchange whilst circulation of both fell dramatically, threatening their existence. Thus began the Shells Scandal, the first of a series of events which supposedly brought down the Liberal government.

A fair barometer of Conservative thinking may be HA Gwynne of the Morning Post who wrote a rather revealing letter on 11 May.[7] It was to the Conservative grandee and avowed compulsionist, Lord Milner, a man of great influence in the party. The day before, Milner had sent Gwynne a suggestion that Lloyd George could be flattered and impressed with the necessity for conscription. Gwynne's opinions had moved on from his previous neutrality to compulsion:

'...I agree with you that Lloyd George is the only man who might carry Conscription, and I am becoming more and more of opinion that conscription, far from being distasteful to the people at the moment, would be heartily welcomed....I am only putting it forward now as the only remedy for I feel sure that in this matter the government is behind, and not in front of the people...:

On 13 May Gwynne wrote a leading article, the first part of which wanted enemy aliens interned, but the second part of which was a call for the immediate adoption of universal military service. Gwynne had focused the minds of the Conservative compulsionists and brought into open discussion that which Bonar Law was opposed to. This may be seen as the spearhead of a revolt by half of the Conservative party.

Walter Long wrote to Gwynne on 13 May in fulsome terms:

'Congratulations on your leading article today. Personally I believe the formation of a National government, not a coalition, would be the best thing. It should not exceed fourteen and would have to include all parties. However I don't suppose this is in the range of practical politics.'[8]

This suggestion of a sort of Committee of public safety to deal with the emergency implied the suspension of democratic forms for the duration of the war - a dangerous idea to be batting about in a parliamentary democracy. Gwynne replied next day:

' *As you know, I have not been in favour of a coalition and I hate the idea, but, of course, once the government ask for help, we are in a position where it is quite impossible to refuse it...* ' [9]

In the evening of 14 May, at the suggestion of Lord Robert Cecil; a meeting of the Shadow Cabinet was called to discuss the threat to its position from their own back-benchers. The obvious way to deal with the strengthening revolt was to put themselves at the head of it. To stamp their authority they had to take a strong position towards the government, so it was decided to draft a letter to Asquith urging a more vigorous prosecution of the war; the issue they all agreed upon as needing attention was not the shell scandal - and not Fisher's resignation, which had not yet occurred, nor even the general conduct of the war - but conscription which was now the issue that had come to dominate Conservative thinking.

Apparently the Conservative leaders wished to force the hand of the Cabinet yet offer support for conscription, thus giving the issue a non-party legitimacy:

'In our view...it is impossible to exclude the possibility that it may become necessary...to adopt some form of compulsory organisation with the object of inducing men in some cases to join the Army, and in others, when they are specially qualified, to render not less valuable service in our factories and workshops ... We are without information ... and therefore we are not in as good a position as the Government to judge whether the time has come for an attempt to completely organise the nation for the purposes of the war ... we believe that they will also have the support of the nation. '[10]

This dramatic U-turn by the party leadership, unhappy as many were about compulsion, was taken in the absence of Walter Long who was again ill and shut up in his house at Rood Ashton in Wiltshire. His absence was, for Bonar Law, fortuitous, for Long could not control what was happening, perhaps from his sick bed. Their suggestion for the government was very tentative, for as they added a codicil that they simply did not have enough information to judge whether compulsion was necessary or not. This was not stuff that destroys governments. After the meeting Bonar Law wrote to Long:

about as unsatisfactory as it could be and thought we all were distressed at our helplessness. In the face of such a position we\came to the conclusion that there was nothing we could do except to write Asquith asking him definitely whether the government was\ taking the steps necessary to put into operation a system of compulsory organization which Haldane had himself stated the Gvt regarded as a necessity which might arise. Lansdowne and I are sending a letter to that effect...I think you are right in considering that a coalition may become necessary...I do not think we should agree to it unless the new gvt were constituted in such a way that we could feel that we should really be able to have an effective influence on the conduct of the war...' [11]

The Lansdowne House statement was an extremely significant document, because the Conservative leadership had agreed to put pressure on the government on a specific issue. It was not shells, not shortages, not Kitchener, not the conduct of the war, but Compulsion and that was what Bonar Law was mandated to do by his colleagues. They further promised to support the government in this issue if it brought in conscription - a continuance of patriotic opposition. Lord Robert Cecil had suggested asking for a closed House discussion on several matters that were causing anxiety but they rejected that idea. [12] Their own backbench was furious and Professor Hewins of the UBC, without consulting Bonar Law, wrote a letter to Asquith laying out his dissatisfaction with the conduct of the war, and later a note to signify his intention to ask a question in the House. This was exactly what the Shadow Cabinet had agreed *not* to do. Hewins might have been indignant, and might have been a seeming rising star in the Conservative party, but he was no threat to Asquith. When push came to shove he was just another angry back-bench opposition MP. The only real danger he posed was if he had the backing of someone far more powerful in what he did. If that powerful person behind the scenes was Walter Long, then he was in direct opposition to his party leaders.

In view of the impending court case scheduled for June in Glasgow involving Jacks & Co, an entry in Hewins' diary is intriguing. Against his advice, Hewins' associates approached Bonar Law to urge him to take action, but Bonar Law:

'...gave...a private reason for not taking action...' [13]

The letter to Long is also significant, because Long both did - and did not - want a coalition government. Quite what the difference was between

116

the national government he told Gwynne was needed, and a coalition, is not easy to explain. Bonar Law appeared to think that Long wanted a coalition whereas Long wanted a national government where the country was run by fourteen men from all parties. His notion was for a much more authoritarian body than a mere coalition. Given the implications of that, perhaps Bonar Law, if mistaken in what Long wanted, cannot be blamed for misunderstanding.

Walter Long now had Bonar Law on the ropes; his leader had been forced into a course of action, advocating compulsion, that he had repeatedly resisted, and had, de facto, lost control of the party. Long, according to Lord Beaverbrook was the 'chief of revolt' though the press baron also thought Long had strength of character without firmness of purpose[14] and that he quite often had two contradicting opinions at the same time without realizing it.

Long wrote to Bonar Law in very strong terms correcting his notion that a coalition might be necessary; the letter is undated but is possibly 16 May:

'I desire to state quite plainly that, in my judgment, a coalition is a practical impossibility.... the position does not seem to me to be a bright one, inasmuch as the Prime Minister starts by retaining in the hands of the existing Government the Office of Prime Minister, Foreign Secretary, Secretary for War, and apparently Lord Chancellor and Home Office; which means that the Opposition, if they come in, will unquestionably occupy an inferior position... Would it not be better to tell the Prime Minister that the practical difficulties...are overwhelming and that... the successful and vigorous prosecution of the war is not likely to be attained by the formation of a coalition administration? On the other hand, we, the Opposition, are ready to come to terms with the government; they are in difficulties; they are afraid to face a debate upon munitions of war; our terms are .... [1. Compulsion for Army service and Labour with possible martial law. 2. A more vigorous Aliens policy. 3 Reorganize the War Office to help Kitchener.] This, I am convinced, would be the better policy, and I most earnestly hope that our leaders will consider it before committing themselves to a Coalition government which would, I believe, tend rather to weaken the war administration, while I cannot see how it is possible to avoid the complete destruction of our party as an ultimate consequence.'[15]

Long was not just offering personal advice; neither was he calling to his leader's attention matters which must surely have already occurred to Bonar Law. If the last sentence of his letter is not to be read as hyperbole, then it must be seen as a clear threat that if Bonar Law did not act, then Long would do so. On the shortage of shells and men he also said to Bonar Law on 16 May:

' *I venture to suggest for your consideration whether it might not be well to indicate these views to Asquith and to say that we feel so strongly on the subject that if the government are not prepared to act, we must put down a motion to this effect and ask for a day. I believe this would force his hand, but if it did not, and we abstained from a division, which we could very properly do on the grounds that more than half our men are away at the front, we should, at all events, have made the position clear; and I believe the country would follow our lead and force the government into doing what I believe to be absolutely necessary if the war is to be successfully prosecuted.* '[16]

Long was suggesting active opposition, as opposed to the patriotic opposition which Bonar Law had been following since September – a reversal of policy. What he wanted to do was threatening the breakup of the party, a shattering of the appearance of national unity and a smash-up and a division of the nation. It was also a direct challenge to the authority of Bonar Law.

If that meant the destruction of the Conservative Party as it fell apart into its factions then it appears to have been something that Long had been considering as a possibility. Since he was the 'chief of revolt' then it would be he leading the split - and thus challenging Bonar Law. Some among the 100 Lords and 120 MPs who followed him were pressing for immediate action and had been for some time, HA Gwynne was in communication with Long who thus had at least one newspaper with him:

'*I do think that the opposition ought to begin to move now* '[17]

Gwynne's line in his editorials followed Long's thinking entirely on the twin concerns of shells and compulsion. Long had written to him the previous day:

' *I quite agree that the time has come for the opposition to do something definite. I think we are all of one mind, but the question is how it is to be done. Personally I feel very strongly, and I am quite willing to write a letter or an Article for publication if you think it of any use. I am quite sure we want compulsion for the Army and for Munitions; I could give you a dozen cases to prove this which have come under my own experience. I am writing to Bonar Law and will communicate with you again...*' [18]

What Long actually wanted, he expressed in a letter to Leo Maxse, editor of *The Conservative National Review* magazine, another influential journalist he was in regular communication with. He was against coalition because a 'pro-Boche' party would emerge who wanted to end the war; a coalition would become callous and careless, but with an active Unionist opposition the government could be stirred up. [19]

The storm which would be caused by equivocating over the issue of compulsion would surely have been enough to sweep Bonar Law away. To see Long's threats of mid May 1915, for such they were, as inconsequential would have been foolish of Bonar Law. Beaverbrook saw Long as the main focus for the backbench pressure on Bonar Law, and so he was if anybody was; he was the only figure with sufficient political clout at that time to be so.

Bonar Law was already estranged from many of the unionist rank and file who did not share hiss position on drink. Apart from the fact that he was a teetotaller, 19 out of 23 MPs listed as having links with the brewing industry were Unionists, and five of these were active in the Unionist Business Committee, of which Walter Long was the Chairman. His stance on drink was not popular in his party, and moreover it was against the interests of many brewers who supported the Conservative Party. Now Long was pressing for compulsion and a range of other wishes. Patriotic opposition was about to turn into open criticism and active opposition.

The sheer futility of challenging the government in Parliament was all too plain. Asquith had a majority in the House and any attack on the government that came to a vote of confidence would go down like Cardigan's troopers at Balaklava. Bonar Law would fail, and having failed he would be even more vulnerable, and his party would be damaged in the country as people would be angry that he had attacked the government in wartime; exactly what did happen when Asquith attacked the government in 1918 in the Maurice Debate.

Caught between Walter Long, his antipathy to compulsion, certain defeat in Parliament if he adopted active opposition, drink, the SS Themis and her cargo of possible resignation and disgrace for his family and himself, Bonar Law must have wondered what on earth he was to do next.

The End of the Liberal Government

The events following 14 May 1915 as Professor Koss said in 1968, are bedeviled by a smokescreen.[20] It becomes obvious to any scholar who attempts to study them that the collections of relevant papers in archives and depositaries which deal with this period have been deliberately and willfully weeded out and destroyed. One thing that has emerged since then is that the traditional Beaverbrook version of the end of the last Liberal government simply will not do. It does not stand up to scrutiny.

Fisher, the First Sea Lord, had sent his resignation to Asquith on the morning of 15 May, ostensibly over his disagreement with the Dardanelles campaign and particularly with Winston Churchill. Fisher then disappeared without explanation, and when finally traced, about to take a train for Scotland, he obstinately refused to reconsider. Asquith was not at first worried - Fisher had 'resigned' so many times before. Indeed any notion of Asquith being depressed by Venetia Stanley's engagement which he learned of on 12 May must be set against Violet Asquith writing in her diary that her father could not help laughing at the comic aspects of Fisher's sudden decamping in pulling down all the blinds in his house and laying a red herring trail pointing to Scotland in order to find a place to hide.[21] He apparently then went to earth in the Charing Cross Hotel, just across Trafalgar Square from the Admiralty. To judge from Maurice Hankey's remark in his diary on 13 May, Asquith might have been slightly relieved that Fisher had 'resigned' again:

' *Everyone seems terribly depressed except me - but there is a horrible muddle with all this bickering and intriguing between Churchill and Fisher. Why cannot all work for their country honestly? I am sick of them.*' [22]

Hankey thought that his own exasperation probably reflected a general impression about Churchill and Fisher in the inner circles of the government. The campaign in the Dardanelles was not going well, the original naval assault having failed, necessitating the landing of troops on 24 April. The Prime Minister was aware that the opposition, should they choose, could make much political capital from the Dardanelles situation and Fisher's resignation over it, whatever reply he could make, if the old admiral's decision was definite. An acrimonious debate could well split the fragile appearance of unity in the nation, but Fisher had withdrawn his 'resignation' before.

On Sunday 16 May Asquith was at his country house, the Wharf, in Oxfordshire when Churchill drove over and told him that Fisher meant it and that his resignation was real this time. He offered to resign himself but Asquith did not wish it at that time.

If he was seeking some form of coalition then this was a propitious moment for it to come into being; what happened next has been the subject of some debate, the general tenor of which has been to the effect that Bonar Law forced Asquith into coalition in order to avoid embarrassment over the twin issues of Fisher's resignation and the shell shortage. This version cannot stand because neither of these issues was sufficient to bring down the government, as Martin Pugh has shown.[23] Volumes have been written about the significance of the Shells Scandal and of Fisher's resignation, but in reality, although they increased pressure on Asquith to react, they are actually irrelevant to his final decision. As Pugh has pointed out, all Asquith had to do was to defy the Conservatives with his Liberal, Labour and Irish majority. Over shells and Fisher, ultimately they could not touch him if he did not wish them to.[24] This was true, even of compulsion, but compulsion was what the Conservative Party leaders agreed to press the government on, albeit very mildly.

Asquith had enough information at his disposal, as he subsequently showed in 1919, to demolish any criticism over the supply of ammunition.[25] If that did not work, he had the monumental prestige of his Secretary of State for War to shelter behind.

Any outrage over Fisher's resignation could easily be weathered by producing Fisher's record. His cupidity and monomaniacal tendencies, were only too well evidenced in his own writings and actions, both before and after his resignation. Not long before, he had advocated the shooting of German prisoners and causing some to wonder if he was suffering mental aberrations; Asquith himself wondered this to Lord Stamfordham on 19 May after Fisher wrote to him demanding dictatorial powers over the Navy.[26] This resignation was the ninth of the year, which did not indicate stability of mind, or reliability. If all else failed Asquith could fall back on a parliamentary majority enhanced, as many Tories often bemoaned, by the fact that more of their members had joined the forces than had Liberals; in any vote he could not be defeated. He did not actually have to react at all and just ride out any ineffective storm that the Conservatives might raise. As Maurice Hankey observed:

'A less patient leader than Asquith might easily have lost his head and given way to active resentment but this was not his way...' [27]

The sequence of events, though analysed many times, is unimportant; 139 Conservative MPs were on active service by January 1915 and 41 Liberals, 1 Labour man and 3 Nationalists.[28] Asquith, with a sure majority, did not have to give in to any demands for coalition or anything else if he did not wish to. His position was utterly secure and the Conservatives would lose any vote in the Commons.

On the morning of Monday 17 May 1915 Bonar Law, having heard of Fisher's resignation, went to the Treasury to see Lloyd George - a man who had made no secret of his liking for the notion of coalition. The two men were quite good friends and liked each other as is very plain from the long and affectionate description of Bonar Law in Lloyd George's *War Memoirs*.[29]

Bonar Law wished apparently to continue a conversation that had started the previous evening in the presence of McKenna which had been a rather general one about the shell shortage, and the conduct of the war; now Fisher's resignation had entered the situation. Bonar Law was concerned at the resignation of Fisher and spoke of the impossibility of Churchill remaining at the Admiralty if Fisher had resigned. He made it clear that the opposition would force a challenge about this matter in Parliament, as soon as they knew. He did not mention Long, but he would not be able to halt Long and his friends.

At this point Lloyd George could have shrugged, smiled, mentioned the Liberal majority, and shown him the door. They could have talked all they liked about Fisher - in the end it would come to a vote and the Conservatives could not win it as Bonar Law well knew, and as Long had indicated in his letter the day before. Except that this is not quite what had happened. The truth is probably there, in plain sight. Lord Beaverbrook chronicled this:

' ...Bonar Law was going to tell Lloyd George that if Fisher had really resigned, the Tory party would not permit Churchill to turn Fisher out and remain himself...He pointed out to Lloyd George that Fisher was the

darling of the Tory party. Churchill had become its bugbear. Was the first to go and the second to stay? The rank and file of the Opposition would not tolerate it. When the House met again on Monday the new list of the Admiralty Board would have to be read out. Then the tempest would break with uncontrollable violence and the Opposition would once again begin to oppose. Bonar Law finally told Lloyd George plainly that of his own personal knowledge he was convinced that he could not hold his followers back, even if he wanted to. [30]

This has often been interpreted as a threat. It is not.

It is an admission, of his own weakness and of his own inability to control his own party. Bonar Law knew that his control of his party was a tenuous thing now and that much depended on his appearing to lead. He was a mild mannered man, and nowhere was this more apparent than in his remark to Asquith as they walked into the state opening of Parliament in 1912:

' *I am afraid I shall have to show myself very vicious, Mr Asquith, this session. I hope you will understand*' [31]

The 'pistol' of 17 May 1915 was no such thing. It was a statement of regret- that he was forced into a position that he did not wish to be in - that he was going to have to lead an active opposition, and if he did not, then his position as Tory leader was, in fact, impossible - which it was. On the evening of 17 May an article appeared in the Liverpool Echo which reported a meeting held by the Liverpool Conservative Association that day. They spoke of the advantages of a coalition government, gave their opinion that it would be a good thing to see Bonar Law, Walter Long, FE Smith, Chamberlain and Lord Derby in the Cabinet, and this was days before any suggestion that there would be a coalition was given to the public. They also thought that a nation at war could not be disciplined by a party government but had to be under a national party and a nation government. They then passed a resolution of confidence in Bonar Law. [32] That they felt the need to do so is indicative of stresses within their ranks; it also demonstrates that some Conservatives already felt the need for coalition.

There is something else to consider. The 18 May edition of *The Evening Telegraph and Post*, a Dundee based newspaper, carried the following article which has significance:

123

'TRADING WITH THE ENEMY. THE CHARGE AGAINST GLASGOW MERCHANTS

'The trial has been fixed for June 14 in the High Court of Justiciary, Edinburgh of the four Glasgow merchants who are charged with a breach of the trading with the enemy Act. A pleading Diet will be held in the Sheriff Court, Glasgow on Friday May 28. The accused are members of a Glasgow firm. Two of them came before the Sheriff for declaration on the charge on December 4 last, and in February the two others were before the Sheriff in connection with the charge.'[33]

Jack Law's trial date had been fixed, and possibly on the day that his brother is supposed to have been in a position of such strength that he forced the Prime Minister's hand. Even if the trial date was not fixed on 17 May, then it was done on 18 May and Bonar Law must have known it was about to happen. At this date Jack Law was still one of the accused, yet ten days later when indictments were actually served on two of Jacks' directors, he was not one of them - and neither did he have to appear at the Pleading Diet which was in fact held on 2 June. He was no longer accused despite the fact that he had been under investigation since November, had been arrested in February, and must have expected to go on trial. His position, made clear at the trial, was that he was not an active director of the company any more, and had never had anything to do with iron ore, he being concerned with the steel trading arm of the company. He must have said that previously, yet it had not been accepted and he still faced trial by 18 May. Ten days later his brother was Colonial Secretary in a new coalition government and Jack Law no longer faced trial but was a witness in the trial of his fellow directors.

Regional newspapers often syndicated news articles among themselves; a search in the newspaper archives often finds the same article in paper after paper. Sometimes, as with the eventual Jacks Trial in June, the detail of these articles is very great. Yet this small piece only appeared in *The Evening Telegraph and Post*, in Dundee, which was then a Liberal newspaper. The use of the phrase 'the four Glasgow merchants who are charged' suggests that the reader is supposed to be familiar with the case from previous reports. Yet a search reveals nothing of any previous reports; it is not beyond legitimate speculation that this tiny paragraph escaped the censor, but it does make it clear that at the time he was supposed to be bringing down the government, Bonar Law must have been emotionally fraught. If it is legitimate to bring Asquith's emotional upset

124

over Venetia Stanley into consideration in the fall of the administration, then it is infinitely more so to bring Bonar Law's state of mind into it too, unless of course he felt nothing at all, but that is rather unlikely. It has been a theory since the 1960s that Asquith was so upset by the end of his 'affair' with Venetia Stanley that he gave in to Bonar Law and ended his government. How much more of an emotional strain was there on a Conservative Party leader whose brother and family firm were about to face charges of trading iron ore with the Germans? Particularly when the news was common talk inside Westminster, had been since the beginning of the year, and had caused some speculation about his leadership being able to continue.

To dismiss the Jacks case as irrelevant is not a good idea in this examination.

It is especially not a good idea if the way the Conservatives had behaved over the Marconi Case, and were still behaving over Lord Haldane, is borne in mind. However innocent or otherwise Bonar Law might or might not have been, this affair laid him open to a deadly attack from his political opponents.

Bonar Law then, had just told Lloyd George straight and plain, that he had lost control of his party. He said that the situation was 'impossible', and so it was for him, and on several counts.

What was really said may never be known. Bonar Law apparently talked of getting rid of Churchill if Fisher persisted in his resignation, but of course he was in no position to force that either. At the end of their talk Lloyd George apparently said that the situation was impossible and of course there must be a coalition and went to see Asquith. The only 'of course' here is that the decision was not Lloyd George's to take, and he could not possibly have said it unless he knew that he was pushing on an open door.

Both Beaverbrook and Lloyd George described a sequence where Lloyd George left Bonar Law, went to see Asquith, returned, collected Bonar Law and took him to see the Prime Minister.

RJQ Adams used Austen Chamberlain's account to construct a different sequence where Bonar Law went off, consulted with Lord Lansdowne and Chamberlain, then returned to Downing Street.[34] This in turn built on the sequence set out by Peter Fraser in 1982.[35] Lloyd George,

125

many years later, drew on Beaverbrook's account and it became, for many, the definitive account of what had happened. Yet Beaverbrook was not even in the country when the events unfolded so was no primary witness. Austen Chamberlain said that Bonar Law came to see him after his talk with Lloyd George and that he only went off to Downing Street after Asquith personally telephoned him and invited him to come.[36]

Again the sequence does not actually matter. What does matter is that Bonar Law saw Asquith in a room at 10 Downing Street, and at the end of that meeting Asquith agreed to dissolve the Liberal government and form a coalition. History has represented this, following Lord Beaverbrook's phrase, as Bonar Law pointing his metaphorical pistol at Asquith's head and forcing him to do as he wished him to. It makes no sense.

Two men went into a room with a third, who was junior to one of them. One man was a Prime Minister with a secure majority in the House, complete control of his Cabinet, no contenders for his place apparent in the near future, with a secure mandate and the backing of the Liberal press. One who furthermore habitually exhibited an utter disregard for what the Conservative press said and for which he had an utter disdain, especially in the persons of Lord Northcliffe and HA Gwynne. He consulted no-one else and took the decision entirely on his own, sure in his ability to carry it through.

The other man was leader of his party in default of two others, who really led the two main factions of his party. His speech of resignation had been written because his brother was about to be tried for trading with the enemy. He could, with legitimacy, be accused of profiting from that trade because he had money deposited at interest in the company that had traded with the enemy, his own family firm. Hysterical anti-German rioting was taking place across the nation and any hint that he was linked to something like the Jacks affair could ruin him. His party had just revolted against his authority and forced him to reverse his position on compulsion. Powerful elements of his party, seemingly, were against coalition and wished to change his policy from patriotic opposition, to active opposition, which he did not wish to do because he was a patriotic man who wished to support the government at war, and help if he could. He also knew that the Conservatives could be greatly damaged in the country if they did attack the government in wartime. Furthermore he was being railroaded into a trial of strength in the House that he knew he could not win, and which he would emerge from with his leadership probably damaged beyond repair.

126

There was no pistol in his hand, but there was one at ***his*** head, and Walter Long held it. Asquith, Bonar Law and Lloyd George spoke for about 15 minutes.

There was only one thing that could save Bonar Law. He had to come out of that meeting with Asquith looking like Superman. And the only way this could happen was if Asquith helped him to look that way.

This is not such a strange idea. Bonar Law's 1912 remark showed that he was very aware of how important appearance was to a Conservative leader. As we have seen, Asquith had been demonstrating all the way through, since the start of the war, that he was not averse to working with the opposition. He already had Balfour working with him, and Chamberlain with Lloyd George giving advice at the Treasury. Henderson for Labour was advising him; Kitchener was by repute a Tory, and Bonar Law himself had 'thoroughly enjoyed' attending the War Council in March. With Churchill vociferously in favour of coalition, with Lloyd George supportive of it, and with the notion of it a buzzword around Westminster, Asquith had to have thought about it.

That Asquith gave way to a threat from Bonar Law, who was in no position to threaten, or that he gave way because he was upset at the break up of his relationship with Venetia Stanley, as Roy Jenkins suggested, is highly unlikely. By 19 May he was already writing letters to his next 'muse' Sylvia Henley, Venetia's sister. The theory of Asquith's emotional upset also disregards the way in which Asquith, like so many high level politicians, compartmentalised his life quite ruthlessly, there being a time for work, a time for play, a time for sleep and so on. It also probably misunderstands Venetia's function in Asquith's life, and the romantic one is not necessarily the most important. Asquith tossed his thoughts with Venetia. Or at least some of them - more than he did with anyone else. It is true that there was a lecherous aspect to the relationship, but the nature of their association is so uncertain that it would be a great assumption to hang the failure of the Liberal government on it as a major factor. Venetia knew this, writing to Edwin Montague only three weeks before 17 May - on 20 April:

'I know quite well that if it hadn't been me, it would be someone else or a series of others who would have made him just as happy'[37]

Venetia was his idealised woman, his hetaera, his educated goddess to whom he could confide - and when she was gone he soon, within a

127

fortnight, created another in the shape of her happily married sister Sylvia. And not long afterwards he formed another friendship with Hilda Harrison, and also with Lady Kathleen Scott. So why did he appear to give in and form a coalition? Because he wanted to, as he himself said:

'But it was not merely a question of the particular situation with which we were at the moment confronted. That situation, in one form or another, was certain of recurrence, and I had come to the conclusion that the best chance of an effective prosecution of the war was at once to admit leading men of all parties in the state to a share in the councils and responsibilities of Government [38]

By forming a coalition government he gained a hatful of glittering prizes, and avoided something rather annoying that could have turned out badly.

Firstly, he would gain the continued cooperation of the opposition and avoid fractious debates in the Commons. He found it a great relief, as he had told Venetia, when the House was not sitting, and in fact the House had not sat very much since the beginning of the war.

Secondly, with the opposition on his side, the Conservative press would be happy and cease their campaigns against him, notably on Shells and on Fisher. This was an issue according to Jack Pease the Education Minister who wrote:

'... quite apart from the Winston-Fisher episodes Asquith had been feeling for quite a while that he would be compelled to make the Tories assume a share of responsibility because of the horrible campaign now being carried on by Harmsworth and other papers [39]

Plainly, if this is true, Asquith's protestations that he took no notice of the Press were a little strained.

Thirdly, Bonar Law was weak politically, his position needed bolstering, and the shape of the new government would therefore be determined by Asquith and dominated by the people he appointed. Bonar Law could not do this because he had never held Cabinet rank.

Fourthly, Bonar Law was weak in his party; Asquith did not wish to see someone like Walter Long take over the Conservative leadership because Long was very popular in his party, powerful in the country and the media and could make life very difficult for him.

Fifthly, and very importantly, the mandate of the government was due to run out at the end of November 1915 and if Asquith was to avoid calling an election in wartime, when many of the electors were away on active service and many of the current

MPs as well, he had to reach an accommodation with the opposition. That it was very much a talking point on 17 May is well illustrated by an article which appeared in *The Yorkshire Evening Post*, but which was syndicated around newspapers throughout the UK:

'Much has been heard from time to time of the difficulty of holding a General Election while the war is in progress…One point has been decided - there will be no formal General Election… the idea was discussed but set aside on the ground that, if all parties are agreed that the life of this Parliament should be prolonged they should take steps accordingly without putting the country to the trouble and expense of a meaningless General election… It may now be assumed, therefore that the attention of party leaders is now directed to the period and conditions of extension of the present Parliament… '[40]

An opportunity for such an accommodation walked into Downing Street admitting he could no longer control his party; Asquith leaped at his chance.

Sixthly, as Martin Pugh pointed out in 1974, if Asquith proposed a coalition then he would, and did, face opposition from his own party who would, quite reasonably, wish to fight it out with the Conservatives. If a situation arose where he was able to bounce them into one, then he would obviate the need for explanation; the shells shortage headlines and the resignation of Fisher gave him the perfect opportunity for such a bounce - and he never did explain why, even when faced with 100 furious Liberal MPs on 19 May shortly after the announcement of the coalition.[41]

Seventh, Asquith was able to split the Conservatives into a group who cooperated with him, and another who did not, but were now muzzled because their own leaders were in the government.

Eighth, Asquith was already the leader of what was de facto, a coalition. He was Prime Minister because he had the support of the Labour Party and the Irish Nationalists, and without them he would fall. They might have no formal responsibility in his administration, but they could end it at any time they wished. Offering an expanded coalition did not alter this if refused, but if accepted then he could bring both within the fold. In the end he failed to tempt the Nationalists in, but Labour did enter the new coalition.

Ninth, but probably least importantly, Asquith said afterwards that negotiations to induce Italy to enter the war on the Allied side were at a critical phase and he did not wish to give them an appearance of disunity in Britain, which might put them off. However, Italy had already renounced her obligations to the Triple Alliance and signed the Treaty of London in April 1915 - she declared war on 23 May whilst the new coalition was being formed in Britain. Internal government wrangling at this stage would probably not affected events.

Tenth and lastly, this situation presented Asquith with the opportunity to extend his ministry far beyond the terms of his election mandate without facing a further election, and rendering a wartime election not necessary. That he was able to extend his administration for a full year beyond its legal expiry date must surely be seen as an achievement worthwhile having, There are, after all, very few Prime Ministers who have had the chance to rule the UK without being elected.

The most important of these points, the fifth, was the life of Parliament, which HA Taylor said in his 1932 biography of Bonar Law:

'...the necessity of avoiding a General election when the life of the present Parliament should expire, brought the two Unionist chiefs to Downing Street. Gradually it became clear beyond a doubt that a Coalition was inevitable. Much has been written of the circumstances in which ultimately the steps were taken. Interesting, and in some respects piquant, as were the circumstances attending the formation of the First Coalition, they matter little to History. Such a development was natural, logical and, if anything, overdue...'[42]

Taylor, like Bonar Law, saw the alternative as an impossible situation where everyone with a grievance could come forward to use opposition to his own ends. Bonar Law always tried to avoid discussions that might be of service to the enemy but found himself on 17 May in an impossible situation fraught with all kinds of potential menaces to the successful prosecution of the war. This was not purely the wisdom of hindsight either. Lord Sandhurst, who retained his post had remarked on it in his diary on 26 May:

'Enter the National Cabinet; I am not very much in love with the general idea, but perhaps it was inevitable. The opposition could not govern with the present House of Commons majority and an election is impossible...' [43]

What would be annoying and nasty for Asquith and the country would be that if the Conservative press united against him, then the clamour against his government would make for great distractions in running the war, and would split national unity, which was a thing to be fostered and guarded. It would lower the prestige and popularity of the government, which, of itself, would not help national unity. Worse, if the Conservatives switched, as they were apparently doing, from patriotic opposition to active opposition, then much energy and time would be spent countering it, and the enemy would be greatly encouraged by seeing the splits in their opponents' ranks.

Going into a form of coalition with Bonar Law was, in reality, what might be termed a 'no-brainer'. All that Asquith had to do was tell his party, and make them accept it, which he did, and the small amount of fuss was quashed mercilessly and quickly. Then he could tell everyone, as he always did, that the coalition was suggested by Bonar Law, and make a few sacrifices to make it look real. Obvious choices for the latter were Haldane, whom press hysteria was making out to be some sort of traitor, and whose popularity in the country was at rock bottom, and Churchill, who could not remain at the Admiralty because so many Conservatives disliked him and championed Fisher. Lloyd George apparently told Churchill that he threatened to resign if Asquith did not agree to a coalition, but he is the only source for this assertion. [44] Asquith himself did not have to be particularly happy about what he was doing; the fact is that it was necessary; he could see the necessity and so he would do it. In the case of Haldane Asquith resisted pressure from both Edward Grey, who also agreed that a coalition was necessary, and from the King, both of whom wished Haldane to remain in the government, but his ruthlessness is perhaps revealing in its determination. The demotion of Churchill and the dropping of Haldane from the new government gave veracity to the story that Bonar Law had forced Asquith's hand. However his greatest problem now lay in the choosing of his new ministers, the selection of whom was completely at his disposal.

Bonar Law's problem was far worse.

Chapter 8

In which Mr Long Decides to be of Service

Bonar Law's task after his meeting with Asquith on 17 May was to bring the united Conservative Party into a coalition when he knew that many if not most in his own party were against it.

No-one left any account of what happened in the short meeting between Asquith, Bonar Law and Lloyd George, and no-one knows who suggested coalition first, but given Bonar Law's position, any threat from him would have been laughed at over the Prime Minister's departing shoulder. Asquith agreed to coalition inside 15 minutes because he wanted one. The suggestion must be that Asquith had wanted this very thing to happen for some time. Nothing else is satisfactory in explaining the alacrity with which he acted.

As Bentley Gilbert showed in his biography of Lloyd George, Asquith's decision took about 15 minutes.[1] As Pugh has pointed out, this indicates, given the character of Asquith, that he had evidently given the matter prior thought.[2] Pugh also drew attention to the fact that Bonar Law was always at pains to say that the initiative came from Asquith, and not himself. Bonar Law's famous 'ultimatum' was in fact an agreed form of words between Asquith, Lloyd George, and himself; the only possible conclusion, since there is a carbon copy in the Asquith Papers of Bonar Law's statement, typewritten and dated the day before he gave Asquith his note. There is yet another copy in Lloyd George's papers with the following note by it:

'Dear LLG I enclose copy of the letter. You will see we have altered it to the extent that we do not definitely offer coalition, but the substance is the same.'

Lord Lansdowne and I have learnt with dismay that Lord Fisher has resigned, and we have come to the conclusion that we cannot allow the House to adjourn until this fact has been made known and discussed. We think the time has come when we ought to have a clear statement from you as to the policy which the Government intend to pursue. In our opinion things cannot go on as they are, and some change in the constitution of the Government seems to us inevitable if it is to retain a sufficient measure of public confidence to conduct the war to a successful conclusion. The situation in Italy makes it particularly undesirable to have anything in the nature of a controversial discussion in the House of Commons at present, and if you are prepared to take the necessary steps to secure the object I have indicated, and if Lord Fisher's resignation is in the meantime postponed, we shall be ready to keep silence now. Otherwise I must today ask you whether Lord Fisher has resigned, and press for a day to discuss the situation arising out of his resignation.[3]

This is the famous 'pistol' held at Asquith's head supposed to have brought down the Liberal government. On the face of it, it does not actually demand anything that Asquith had not shown signs of being willing to entertain anyway. He was already involving people of all three parties in his administration Bonar Law was still hesitating over coming out with the 'coalition' word, considering that Walter Long had just told him he was against the idea, but the collusion is quite clear. Bonar Law did not wish to use the word 'coalition' because there was a very good chance at this stage that he would split his own front bench and some of them would be in government whilst some would not be. Persuasion would be necessary.

Chamberlain was also clear that there was collusion; according to him, on 17 May it was:

'Agreed between them that there should be no pubic reference to Mr Bonar Law's letter of that morning (the supposed ultimatum to which Asquith capitulated) but that the starting point of the negotiations was to be taken as the invitation of Mr Asquith to the leader of the Opposition to cooperate in the formation of a National Government.'[4]

On the evening of Monday 17 May Asquith told Margot that Fisher had definitely resigned, but went on:

'I've had to take very drastic measures. I wrote to all my colleagues to resign. I shall form a coalition government. I've just seen Bonar Law. He was pleased and happy; of course they long to be in it.'[5]

It is not surprising that Bonar Law was pleased and happy, in the same way as he had been pleased to be invited to the War Council; his position as leader was secured, he looked like the man who had brought down the government and his authority soared. Asquith also said to Margot that Lloyd George was happy because he had always wanted a coalition, but did not talk about it to outsiders. Given what Asquith had secured, he probably should have been most pleased of all; his tenure of Downing Street, as a result of this, would probably, and ultimately did, continue long beyond the limit of his mandate. Bonar Law's seeming force majeur secured his position in his party, and Asquith was able to face his own people and say that he had responded to irresistible pressure from Bonar Law and acted in the interests of national unity. Certainly the letter he wrote to Lord Stamfordham, the King's private secretary that evening indicates that he was very much in charge:

'...After much reflection and consultation today with Lloyd George and Bonar Law I have come decidedly to the conclusion that, for the successful prosecution of the war, the government must be reconstructed on a broad and non-party basis....' [6]

Read carefully, it is plain that Asquith had thought the matter through. 'Much reflection' did not take place on 17 May - it took 15 minutes, therefore Asquith was stating quite clearly here that he had been thinking about a coalition for some time:

The affair was presented to HA Gwynne as the Liberals asking the Conservatives for help, which they could not refuse. He wrote to Walter Long on 17 May, having heard the news of the coalition, and he favoured it, hoping that Long, of all men, would help to make it a success. [7]

In a leader article of 18 May he set out a shopping list of what the opposition should be asking for as a preliminary if they were to share in the task of government, and such is the list that it is clear he thought the coalition would be dominated by Conservatives and their thinking. He also wrote to the owner of *The Morning Post,* Lady Bathurst, stating that he did not like Coalition, but could not see how it was possible to refuse to help, provided the government was purged of 'rotters'.

Professor WAS Hewins was not fooled by what had actually happened as he wrote on 18 May. There had been no pistol at Asquith's head:

'... though some deny that Bonar Law forced on the change of Govt. Our experience of course is that BL & Co have always- up to the last moment, deprecated and discouraged strong action. My inference from the facts I know, wh. may be mistaken, is that Asquith, when faced with the determined attitude of the Unionists, tried to meet it and prevent attack by putting a few Front Bench Unionists into the ministry and that he had not in view a complete reconstruction'. [8]

He was almost correct. However, it was not Asquith who reacted to determined unionist threats which presented no danger to him at all, but Bonar Law; and Asquith did not 'try' to prevent an attack by putting a few front bench unionists into his ministry - that is in fact exactly what he did do.

Austen Chamberlain wrote to Bonar Law on 17 May in terms that make it quite clear who proposed the coalition idea:

'There are no two ways about it. If our help is asked by the Government we must give it. God knows each one of us would willingly avoid this fearful responsibility; but the responsibility of refusing is even greater than that of accepting and in fact we have no choice.[9]

They had no choice. Asquith probably knew that, and made an offer that they could not refuse.

On 19 May Asquith announced the coming reconstruction of the government in the Commons. He emphasized that no person or body of persons had made anything in the nature of surrender or compromise of their purposes or ideals. It was done solely for the purposes of the war. Bonar Law followed him, but was not at all triumphant, speaking in a subdued and low voice so that several honorable members called out to him to speak up as they could not hear what he was saying.[10] It was not the performance of a man who had forced anyone's hand.

Lord Northcliffe had decided that Kitchener constituted a 'rotter' and had to go in the reshuffle. On 21 May he over-reached himself and demonstrated the limitations of the press at the same time. *The Daily Mail* launched a violent attack on Kitchener and in turn suffered a violent reaction from the public. Viscount Sandhurst, the Lord Chamberlain, noted that the mail was burned on the Stock Exchange floor, the Oxford Union voted to boycott it, and the London Clubs considered not taking the paper any more. Sandhurst[11] thought that Kitchener had started the row by calling Northcliffe to the War Office and telling him what he thought of him and his papers. Kitchener had already refused to allow a *Daily Mail* correspondent at the front; the man in the street apparently was saying that Germany needed no spies in Britain so long as *The Times* and *The Daily Mail* were there. The overall effect was that all sorts of resolutions of confidence rained in for Kitchener and this made his position at the War Office quite safe. His position, for all the talk of plots to oust him, was never really in danger, for his status with the population at large was godlike. Any government who sacked him would have faced severe disturbances, especially in the fevered climate of May 1915.

The matters of Fisher's resignation and the shortage of shells were slipping into the background as matters of coalition and what might be achieved, now took over. As far as the shells shortage is concerned, George Riddell, writing in his diary on 16 May had a fairly clear view of what was going on, writing in his diary on 16 May:

'...it is said that French is acting most disloyally to Kitchener and that the article by Repington which appeared in The Times two or three days ago in which it was alleged that K had neglected to supply the Army with high explosive shells, was inspired by French. It is suggested that French is endeavouring to work up a Press campaign in his own favour,'[12]

Curiously, it was Riddell, in a conversation with Winston Churchill on 19 May who perhaps came closest to answering the question as to why French had acted as he did:

'Do you think that French was justified in causing Repington to write that inspired article regarding shells which appeared in The Times? Should he not have written to the Prime Minister?' Winston replied 'the poor devil is fighting for his life'.[13]

The remark is enigmatic and is not explored any further, although on 21 May Kitchener told Margot that French had seen both Northcliffe and Repington and that Sir John French had done 'this'. He might have been fighting for his professional life, but a press campaign was not going to work against Asquith.[14]

Even more enigmatic was Asquith's speech to a meeting of 100 resentful, angry and vehement Liberal MPs on 19 May, who wondered why on earth he had destroyed their government and delivered them into the hands of Lord Northcliffe and Horatio Bottomley the Editor of John Bull. He opened his speech by telling them that he could not tell them the truth and could only appeal to their love, fidelity, faith and service. It was not the press that had forced him to it, as they well knew, he took no notice of the press.   His authority was formidable - to walk into a room of angry shouting men, his own MPs, the bulk of his majority and make such an appeal, without giving reasons is the surest indicator of how powerful he was in the party; and they accepted what he said.[15]

That Asquith had bounced back fairly well from Venetia's announcement of marriage is attested by a letter of 19 May to his new muse, Mrs Sylvia Henley:

'... a regular mutiny was on foot among our people against the 'coalition'. They got together a meeting in one of the Committee Rooms wh. was attended by almost all the good men on the back benches... and expressed themselves with the utmost freedom; duped by the Government, 'treated like dirty ciphers' etc, etc and proclaimed their intention to debate the whole thing in the House this evening. The situation looked serious and Gulland (Chief whip) implored me to go and beard them, which I promptly did. It was one of the most curious experiences I had ever had; a roomful of old and devoted friends, full of soreness and indignation, and in many cases, of fury. I was of course unable to tell them the whole or even half of the truth so I had to go more for their affections than their reason...[16]

The Liberal radical wing was as desperate as Long, but for different reasons. They firmly believed that Asquith had capitulated as one leading Scottish Liberal recorded when he got home that day. MacCallum Scott's diary observation of 19 May has provided ammunition to those who say Asquith was worn out, tired and past it:

'Asquith announced today that the Government was under reconstruction. Afterwards, at a hastily called party, some spoke very strongly against a coalition, taking the line that the Prime Minister owed some explanation to his party. Asquith was persuaded to address the meeting. He spoke with deep feeling. He looked old and worried. He flung himself on our mercy. The situation was of the gravest kind. Coalition had become inevitable. It was not pleasant to go into harness with men who were his bitterest enemies. He asked for our confidence - he would not let us down. The meeting gave him an over-powering ovation.[17]

The meeting took place in the evening; at 62 years of age, he was entitled to look old. Next morning he would still have looked old, but less tired perhaps. As to worried, he had good cause to be worried; the only thing that could really stop his coalition project was if his own backbenchers opposed it. He offered to resign during the meeting, was very emotional and gained the overwhelming backing of his followers; if his design was to have his men rally to their leader then he succeeded brilliantly. There was no overt opposition from the Liberal Party. In politics outcomes are the sign of the success or failure of policy.

Appearance is perhaps not so important. Asquith may have appeared defeated, had in reality triumphed, but his feigning defeat did him no service in the long term. The myth of his defeat was planted firmly in the minds not only of his enemies, but also his friends. That the Liberal Party was up for a fight demonstrates quite clearly that Asquith did not have to resign. He had a majority in the House whatever happened.

Years later, in *Great Contemporaries*, Churchill had no doubts at all as to who was in control of the whole process:

'When Lord Fisher resigned in May and the opposition threatened controversial debate, Asquith did not hesitate to break his Cabinet up, demand the resignations of all Ministers, end the political lives of half his colleagues, throw Haldane to the wolves, leave me to bear the burden of the Dardanelles, and sail on victoriously at the head of a coalition. Not 'all done by kindness'. Not all by rosewater! These were the convulsive struggles of a man of action and ambition at death grips with events.'[18]

However, it was not until Tuesday 15 June that Asquith spoke to the House of Commons on why the coalition had been formed, and the *Aberdeen Daily Journal* correspondent thought his mood very hesitant.[19] He admitted that the word coalition had not a pleasant savour in British politics and he recalled the disastrous coalitions of Fox, Lord North and Lord Aberdeen, but the present situation was 'without parallel'. As he made this remark he turned to look Mr Bonar Law, sitting beside him, full face and he nodded approvingly. Up to the last moment the Prime Minister was not sure how he could best respond to the call of public duty, and he had found the formation of a national government in order to obliterate even the semblance of a one-sided government, a repugnant task, but he never told the House the full reasons why he had done it. 'A great cause is at stake' was the nearest he got.

He also stated that he had reconstructed the government and desired to say that he should not have been justified in doing what he did under pressure of any transient Parliamentary exigencies. Plainly he had not responded the way he did because of pressure over shells, compulsion, Fisher, fear of debate, but for quite other reasons. He had, as Paul Adelman remarked, performed a brilliant piece of political legerdemain and ensured the continuance of his administration.[20]

Whatever happened in the 15 minute meeting of 17 May with Bonar Law, the Conservative leader came out of the room looking like a winner, a hero; decisive, in charge and very much the man of the moment. In the next few days Lord Haldane was sacked, one of Asquith's oldest friends, Churchill was demoted and this gave the much-needed semblance of veracity to the idea that Bonar Law had used force to bring about a coalition. Haldane had been pilloried so much in the press that the axing of one of Asquith's closest colleagues had to look like a victory to them; a Bonar Law victory. It looked good; and it had to; Bonar Law was not yet out of danger; Walter Long was unconvinced.

Bonar Law had been tasked by his Shadow Cabinet at the Lansdowne House meeting on 14 May with a mild challenge to the government on the subject of compulsion. He had short-circuited this process, which would have ended in defeat by sending a much more general letter than his colleagues intended, and come back with a coalition government, which many did not want. However, it was clear that the compulsionists' concerns could not be ignored with temerity even had Asquith wished to. Some of them were even taking on themselves to speak for 'the army', when they were in fact speaking for themselves, which had rather Cromwellian undertones:

'...The Army will expect that compulsory service will be a condition of your participation in the govt. The declaration of such a policy would, as I said, have the effect of a slashing victory...' [21]

Haldane's statement of 13 May though is a clear indication that the Liberals had no intention of ignoring the possibility of bringing in conscription if it became necessary.

'...Even though we may think that in ordinary conditions in time of peace the voluntary system is one from which it would be most difficult for us to depart, yet we may find that we have to reconsider the situation in the light of the tremendous necessity with which the nation is faced....' [22]

This actually put the broad thrust of the Liberal chiefs' intentions in accord with those of the top Tories; they were not saying 'No' to the idea. So their ideology did not stand in the way. It was a question of necessity, practicality, and timing.

Whatever his intentions might have been, the wind was rather taken out of Walter Long's sails by Bonar Law's accommodation with Asquith, as he wrote on 19 May to Bonar Law:

'I confess that while I have unbounded confidence in Lansdowne and yourself I am very uneasy. I think I may claim to know our party both in and out of the House and I am sure the view of the great majority is that this government are so unscrupulous, so dishonest, that it is almost impossible for two honest English gentlemen, however able they may be, to be even with them.'[23]

Evidently Long was not happy with the deal, but his reasoning was tantalizingly double edged. If sincere, the final sentence is a risible polemic. If not, it could be read as a jibe at Bonar Law for his *naiveté*, or even an implication that they are not up to coping with Asquith and his colleagues. Bonar Law, at any rate, was not remotely English. Whatever his true feelings Long's bluff, if such it was, had been called, any challenge to Bonar Law stifled, and Long would have to make the best of it. Bonar Law's reply to Asquith's note proposing to restructure his ministry, also dated 19 May, has no note of triumphalism, neither does it contain any implication about 'terms':

'Dear Mr Asquith, The considerations to which you refer have for some time been present to the mind of Lord Lansdowne and myself. We have communicated your views and your invitation to our colleagues and we shall be glad to cooperate with you in your endeavour to form a national government.'[24]

He was still hedging his bets and not calling it a 'coalition', perhaps bearing in mind Long's letter of 12 May when he offered to 'stand down' and be solid in favour of Bonar Law if he took part in a 'national government', but then wrote vehemently against coalition on 16 May. By 20 May Long was almost pleading to be heard about what Conservative requirements should be as a price for taking part in a national government.

'I am <u>certain</u> we must have compulsion for army and labour. I <u>believe</u> we ought to have martial law.(sic)[25]

Long's desperate authoritarianism was becoming orthodox on the right wing of the Conservative party, of which he was the 'leader' if anyone had a claim to that position at that time. To Bonar Law, more moderate, it was not - at least not yet; Long's views can scarcely have been any more welcome to Bonar Law than to Asquith; but Bonar Law was the leader and the party would follow him if he gave a decisive lead which he had signally failed to do since September 1914; he was not swayed and agreed to meet Asquith on Saturday 22 May at 11.30am to discuss the allocation of various offices in the new administration. Asquith's note invited Bonar Law, but he had stated to him, possibly verbally, on 20 May that Lansdowne would be welcome to come as well. Given that Lansdowne had supported Bonar Law consistently through the preceding months there was little doubt that he would go along with what was being done. He did not attend the meeting - but Balfour did and took a very great role in it. Bonar Law's note to Asquith indicated that he was carrying his party with him:

'Lord Lansdowne is willing to join in, in view of the strong desire, not only of his old colleagues, but of yourself as expressed to me yesterday...'[26]

John Burns went to the National Liberal Club on 22 May and recorded in his diary what must have been the feeling of the left wing Liberals. They had misread the situation, but perhaps that was not surprising because they were meant to:

'At Club the general impression is that if K of K did what is stated then he should go. If he did not then the PM is guilty of great weakness in surrendering to Tories under the stress of war what they could not otherwise decently claim ...it is defeated via The Times and the Society Anarchist journals like the DM etc, and the PM has capitulated.'[27]

Walter Long was frustrated in his design and continued frantically to agitate to whoever he thought would listen and on 22 May circulated a memo to senior colleagues in the Conservative Party, evidently still hoping that he could head off a coalition and stop it happening. It was virtually a copy of the letter he sent to Bonar Law on the 16 May, except for the line:

'I most earnestly hope that our leaders will consider it before committing themselves to a coalition...'[28]

It repeated the line about how he could not see how it was possible to avoid the complete destruction of *'our party'*. On the face of it this was a frontal attack on Bonar Law's deal with Asquith, because by this date the formation of a coalition government had been public knowledge for four days. He was too late; in his absence Bonar Law had secured the backing he needed from senior Conservatives, particularly Lansdowne and Chamberlain. There were others like Edward Carson and Robert Cecil whose participation he still needed, but in the person of Chamberlain he had the support of at least the Unionist half of his party.

Lloyd George had been putting about the phrase which Beaverbrook used to define the genesis of the coalition about the Tories 'putting a pistol to the heads of the government', but CP Scott was dubious about that, and in salty terms too:

'About the political situation it seems to be that we must take what Lloyd George said as to the Tories 'putting a pistol at the heads of the Government cum grano ...'[29]

He obviously felt that much was hidden, but did not enquire any further. On 23 May, according to Margot, Asquith said that Bonar Law thought leaving Long out of the Cabinet would be more dangerous than including him, as he was the most popular man in the party.[30] Asquith and Bonar Law plainly agreed and when Asquith told Lord Stamfordham with complete frankness on 22 May that some people were being given office, not because they were fitter for office than anyone else, but because they were safer in, than out of office he may have been echoing a conversation about Long with Bonar Law.[31] Long was indeed dangerous - he had been trying to rally support against a coalition by playing on the dislike felt by many Conservatives of Liberal radicals, particularly the Home Secretary Reginald McKenna. He wrote to Bonar Law on 21 May indicating that he had been very active, summoning some of his followers to Rood Ashton, and speaking to others:

'This coalition business is being very badly stage managed.... I have seen some men here, heard from others, and am expressing their views when I say that if McKenna remains in the government the great majority of our men will bitterly resent it and will be scandalized if any of our leaders consent to serve with him'[32]

Considering the influence wielded by Long in the Party, this was a considerable threat. Bonar Law simply did not have the power to decide whether or not McKenna was in the government, and so the coalition idea faltered on what appeared to be the rock of Long's resistance.

Walter Long had a reputation for holding opinions that sometimes contradicted themselves, but considering what he had written about Asquith's government to Bonar Law on 19 May this, to Asquith on 22 May is truly extraordinary:

'...I am satisfied that without compulsion we shall get neither the soldiers we want, nor the munitions of war; and I firmly believe - and I think this must be your view after the debates in Parliament - that the Nation, as regards the vast majority, would heartily approve of its adoption. The real

criticism upon the administration is to be found in this phrase; 'We want to be led; we want to be governed.' In other words it is time for an Autocracy, not for a constitutional government of the ordinary kind and this finds its expression in the adoption of compulsion. The wastage that is going on is appalling. Then many of us think that compulsion would have to be followed by the application of martial law...'(sic) [33]

Exactly what he hoped to achieve by such a letter is hard to fathom. A more complete opposite of the sort of principles Asquith believed in would be difficult to imagine. His letter makes terrifying reading to any Liberal who suspects that behind the mask of Liberal democracy lurks Plato's 'noble lie' - that the idea of government by consent is a thin veneer designed to make acceptable that which is not. What comes through very clearly is Long's terrible sense of frustration and desperation and barely veiled anger; within a week of castigating the government as unscrupulous and dishonest he was trying to 'reason' with the head of that same government, because his entreaties appeared to have no effect on his own leader. The sincerity is genuine, the conviction total and the fervour almost religious; and Long was the acknowledged leader of approximately half of his party whose views he reflected. The twin spectres of compulsion and martial law must have been very real to Asquith and to Bonar Law at the end of a week where troops had to be called out to restore order in London. Once Long's authoritarian solutions were released society could have fractured. There were plenty of people on the left whose views were just as fervent and who were diametrically opposed to all that Long stood for who might have been driven to desperate measures also if Long had had his way at this stage of the war. Long was now a loose cannon smashing about, and in peril of releasing dangerous forces. By forming a coalition Asquith and Bonar Law attempted to contain these forces; perhaps by design, but certainly for convenience. The problem for Bonar Law was how to contain Long and stop his incipient revolt which could see some of his front bench joining a coalition and others effusing, whilst staying in opposition. If the Conservative leader could bring Long onside then the party would fall in behind him and unite behind him. Certainly Long was one of those whom it was more dangerous to leave outside the government than to have in it. The reply came to the letter Long had sent Asquith, but it was not written - a visitor in very human form instead arrived at Rood Ashton to see him on his sick bed on 24 May:

The fall of the Liberal Government and the formation of the first coalition came very suddenly. I was laid up ill, at Rood Ashton, and had made up my mind that, if invited, I would not join the government, as I thought I could be of more use as a private member. I also doubted whether I was in good enough health to be justified in taking office. However, the Chief Whip of our party, Lord Edmund Talbot, came down to see me, conveying a very pressing request from the Prime Minister Mr Asquith, and from my own leader Mr Bonar Law, that I would join the Administration. The Prime Minister showed his invariable kindness and consideration by sending a message to me that I could select one of the offices with which I was thoroughly familiar as this would probably entail less labour than oing to a new department.

Notwithstanding the offer, I told Lord Edmund that nothing would induce me to join the Government, but I would support it with all the power and influence I possessed. Nevertheless he persisted and announced that he would not leave the house till I consented. The result of his perseverance was that I wrote a letter which he took back to the Prime Minister, telling him that I would accept the Local Government Board, of course as a member of the Cabinet.[34]

Long did not mention that Herbert Samuel, President of the local Government Board, whose job Long was offered, also visited him and he was a far more direct link to Asquith.[35]

The question must inevitably arise as to what actually changed Long's mind, for he does not actually say. One speculative possible answer may be found by going forward four days, to the meeting of the new Cabinet on 28 May, which Long attended. Asquith's letter to the King included this:

'The War Office & Bd of Trade were directed to draw up memoranda for circulation to the Cabinet in regard to the actual military and naval situation, to recruiting, and to the supply of, and possibilities of organizing for war purposes, the labour of the country...'[36]

This is exactly what Long had wanted. It is not beyond reason that when Herbert Samuel visited Long on 24 May he conveyed Asquith's offer of the Local Government Board, which position Samuel currently occupied, and an offer to discuss the whole question of labour, recruiting and compulsion at the earliest opportunity. That would be irresistible to him, especially because if he were mounting a threat to Bonar Law on the grounds that he was not pushing compulsion, then Bonar Law had just stolen his clothes. Samuel lost nothing - he was to stay in the Cabinet anyway, and on 26 May he was appointed Postmaster General in place of Charles Hobhouse, who was dumped.

As the cherry on Long's cake he might also have been offered the steering of the putative national register through parliament, because before another month was out, that is what he was doing.

His leadership challenge blunted, the backbench rebellion stifled, Long now had his hands on the levers of power and the chance to push through his own particular obsession into legislation. It was a signal triumph for him, and if this is what was offered on 24 May it is little wonder that he grabbed at it.

Bonar Law was safe. Long was muzzled, the Conservative revolt was over. Bonar Law was now in complete control and looked like the hero of the hour.

Mark Bonham Carter wrote to Violet Asquith on 21 May revealing that the attitude of the Conservatives to each other was interesting. Bonar Law was unhappy about Austen Chamberlain being made Secretary of State for India, a senior post in the Cabinet whilst he was not under consideration for something of at least equal status.

'BL has no illusion about his own position in the party, frankly recognizing that he is a compromise...'[37]

Bonar Law, even at this time, held a tentative balance between the Tory right led by Long, and the Unionist left led by Chamberlain. Now both his potential rivals had accepted office under Asquith. He himself settled for Secretary of State for the Colonies, which, despite the title, was junior to both Chamberlain and Long; this is perhaps a sign that Asquith knew he did not have to try too hard to please Bonar Law. What Asquith and Bonar Law had done was effectively to form a 'party' of the centre - a coalition of the front benches whose sober-minded luminaries combined to contain the threats from their own backbenchers. This was perceived at the time - Francis Hirst, the editor of *The Economist*, a Liberal organ, wrote on 31 May:

'I think the time has come to act without delay in the matter of conscription. I fear that nearly all the Liberal journalists and newspaper proprietors can easily be got at and persuaded. The Liberal Imperialists and the Tory Imperialists together are quite capable of working up a panic

and rushing the country into military slavery....John Burns predicts a revolution in the North.[38]

Yet they had contained illiberal forces which threatened Parliament itself as a legislative body.

Langan and Schwarz pointed out in 1985 that the election of 1910 had balanced the forces within Parliament so evenly that conflicts could scarcely be resolved within it. [39] Instead MPs had taken to forming leagues and groups with people outside Parliament in order to lobby for their own programmes - the Tariff Reform League and the Budget Protest League being among them. The radical right was concerned not so much with opposing the Liberals but with opposing and containing reform movements - the politics of reaction indeed. Langan and Schwarz stated that two prominent right-wing Unionists, Henry Page Croft and Lord Willoughby de Broke, were planning a new National Party in 1911. This idea was shelved when Bonar Law became leader and the issue of Ireland lined up the Conservatives behind him. Lloyd George, when he proposed a coalition government in 1911 was in deep consultation with Edward Carson and Lord Milner. The Conservative party as a whole shifted towards the right, attracted towards belligerent anti-Socialism. Nonetheless, no single cause had enough power to unite the Conservatives and they veered in all directions. Langan and Schwarz pointed to the possibility of Liberal Imperialists joining Unionists to form a party of the centre. In this fluid atmosphere they posited the idea that a situation came into being in British politics which was 'Caesarist'. That is to say that Parliament became 'Caesarist', retreating in the face of radical populism and espousing solutions for national problems which were imposed by policy leaders; these were the 'Caesars'. If Langan and Schwarz were correct then the great temptation for many politicians must have been to play an actual Caesar, or as they were so fond of calling him 'a big man'. There were enough people calling for a 'big man' to come forward and eventually they got him in the shape of Lloyd George in December 1916; to some extent British politics has never recovered from this, because 'good' Prime Ministers are expected to be presidential or Caesarist to this day. The emergence of Long as a Caesar was neatly averted in May 1915 by the formation of the coalition.

This Caesarist tendency was antithetical to new Liberalism and Asquith would have sought to avoid this. Forming a party of moderates to stave off Caesar, by ensuring that centre politics stayed in control, would be

146

an effective measure. In 1915 Asquith and Bonar Law *de facto*, if not *de jure*, did this. They had to conceal the bones of what they had done or the whole fragile edifice would fall apart, with consequences for national unity and the war effort. The most outspoken dissenters had been brought into consultation and could now work out their energies within the framework of legitimate government, with all the checks and balances of Parliament in place.

However, not everyone liked it. John Burns spoke for many on the left of the Liberal party when he placed the blame for the 'fall' of the government squarely on:

'...the apes of Fleet Street as Carlyle called them, the factions and blackguards of Carmelite Street are revealing themselves to their former dupes in impudent role of swashbuckling dictatorship and urging Autocracy for government, Conscription for enlistment and making Europe a shambles as the best and only method of adjusting differences between mankind'.[40]

Burns did not mince words in his diary but the strength of his feeling was not less than that of Long. Even a week later after time to reflect Burns was still fulminating:

'The new coalition is the Old Tory Party writ large with a true blue office pencil. The PM has sold his party, deserted his colleagues, misled his country and destroyed much of his reputation by his surrender to The Times.[41]

The underlining implied that Asquith had sold out in order to maintain himself in office, but the capitalization indicated that Burns believed that the right wing of the Conservative Party was setting the agenda; his bitterness is clear. On 31 May he wrote:

'The Tories having stampeded Government now occupy really all the best offices...Liberals very depressed. Labour doubtful already of inclusion. Irish alone free from entanglements. This Cabinet does not increase efficiency to extent to justify its creation.[42]

Since all the major offices of state stayed firmly in Asquith's hands it has to be surmised that pique was blinding Burns' view of Asquith's coup. Asquith and Bonar Law were not rivals, but colleagues, treading a very delicate path with yawning gulfs on either side. They might not like each other, though their interest coincided for the moment, but Asquith was definitely in charge. The same was true of their ministers, who actually said they did not like sitting with each other - but they did anyway and Asquith was in charge of them too. As to the backbenches on both sides, they were disgusted with the new arrangements but had no choice but to accept what their leaders had done.

Beaverbrook later said that most Conservatives felt 'diddled' when the coalition was put together, and some certainly felt that their own leader had not been given the senior Cabinet post that he should have had; the Prime Minister put together a form of coalition that gave the Liberals maximum advantage and conceded little to the Conservatives. They saw this as unjust given that they thought the Liberals had asked for their help. Beaverbrook put this in his account of what happened in the making of the coalition.

'Bonar Law was well aware of the Liberal design and must have listened with cynical amusement to the appeal to his patriotism which was made in order to reconcile him to the sacrifice of his rights ... he told Asquith "You mustn't think I am doing this because I am compelled to. I know very well that I can have what I want simply by lifting my little finger." '[43]

He almost certainly never said this to Asquith. HA Taylor in his 1932 biography of Bonar Law spoke to many close friends and colleagues of Bonar Law who knew him very well indeed, and he said:

'The mode of expression seems a little unusual for Bonar Law. Possibly it is not intended to be an exact report of his words' [44]

For one it would have been completely out of character, and secondly the quotation was attributed to Bonar Law by Lord Beaverbrook who used it to illustrate what he thought was Bonar Law's attitude. That he did not lift that finger is surely an indication that he did not do so because he did not wish to foment a crisis, despite his so called 'ultimatum'. After Peter Fraser's 1982 exposure of Beaverbrook's habit of fabricating things, making them up and getting his facts and chronology mixed up, it's a reasonable assumption that this is a little piece of embellishment which has received far more weight than it should have.[45]

Bonar Law had passed through a dangerous minefield and his position had been almost intolerable on 17 May. If Asquith had not decided to go for coalition it is hard to see how Bonar Law could have stayed leader of his party with his authority so devastated by a forced change of policy, a forced U-turn on compulsion and a defeat caused by leading his party into a

Commons debate that he could not win. Now his position was safe and he was a member of the Government as Secretary for the Colonies, with Mr squith as his Prime Minister.

Now Long was no longer a loose cannon smashing things up, but safely tethered where he could explode to good effect; he wrote to Bonar Law on 30 May:

'...I thought the Cabinet went off well & I am more hopeful. I think it is clear there has been no cohesion, no initiative, no decision, & that each Minister has been left to hoe his own row - we shall soon alter this - in fact we made a good beginning on Friday - one of the late Cabinet told us they had never got so much from K since the war began! I am not satisfied about men or munitions, we shall I hope have much fuller and more detailed information. We are all very grateful to you for the fine fight you made and the good terms you secured. With K Winston and Lloyd George we shall I think be fairly safe.

My personal and sincere thanks for all you did on my behalf. Walter H Long.'[46]

The only real problem for Bonar Law now was that two directors of his family company, where he had thousands of pounds deposited at interest was about to come up in a trial in Edinburgh, charged with trading with the enemy, and his brother was to appear as a witness.

Disgrace beckoned. Worse, an hysterically anti-German public could turn on him. If any shadow fell on him from the Jacks Affair then many in his party would probably turn on him and his leadership would be over. His government position would also have to be forfeit. The personal and emotional strain on him at this time must have been almost unbearable.

But he was a government minister now; and this was no ordinary trial, not by any stretch of the imagination.

Chapter 9

Trading with the Enemy

On 22 August 1914 the government published a 'clarification' to its hastily passed Trading with the Enemy Act where it made clear certain aspects of the Act which were causing confusion to businesses. Among the points it attempted to clear up was one which stated that commercial contracts entered into before the war started cannot be performed during the war, and payments for anything received already should not be made to such firms during the war. This was widely published in the press, such as *The Western Daily Press* of that date - but it continued:

'Where, however, nothing remains to be done save to pay for goods already delivered or for service already rendered, there is no objection to making the payment... '[1]

This little piece of legal acrobatics then went on to say that the question of whether or not contracts were suspended or terminated was a question of law, which may depend on circumstances, and in cases of doubt British firms must consult their own legal advisors. It is perhaps then no surprise that some companies got caught with their fingers in the cookie jar. To prohibit trading with the enemy seems axiomatic on the outbreak of a war, but it was not as clear-cut and simple as that. With goods delivered - or on the way, orders part fulfilled, payments made and so on, many companies found that they were almost required to stop juggling, yet all their balls were in the air. In other words, if large amounts of money were outstanding, then it could make quite a difference to the survival of the company concerned. As to making prohibition retrospective - people were always going to get caught. Jacks & Co were far from unique. The courts would have to make decisions on individual cases.

One of the first cases heard was on 28 September 1914 when George Newton Spencer, a clerk, was charged with unlawfully inciting Frank H Houlder of Houlder's Shipbrokers, Leadenhall Street London, to trade with the enemy.[2] The defendant was employed by a large German shipping company in Hamburg when war broke out. They had a number of ships in neutral ports when war started and did not wish them to leave those ports for fear of destruction or seizure. They therefore instructed the defendant to see Mr Houlder to make arrangements to pay any moneys due on the ship's mortgages to the owners in Germany. Mr Houlder would then own the ships. Mr Houlder, who held the mortgages of course, reported him for trading with the enemy. The defendant, a Scotsman, had tried several times to speak to someone at the Foreign Office to see if he as acting within the law but had failed to speak to anyone. Bail was refused and he was remanded in custody.

On 14 October Spencer pleaded not guilty before Mr Justice Rowlatt. Mr Muir in prosecuting him said that the accused had been working in Germany and had returned home on 23 September on a passport granted by the American Consul in Hamburg. His German employers thought their ships were no use to them stuck in neutral ports and his mission was to propose to Houlder's that they pay large sums of money to the Germans, take the ships and run them as their own. If the scheme had gone through £28,400 would have been paid to the Germans through a Dutch bank.

Spencer said the Germans would shoot him if he did not succeed and produced an authority from the German government to transfer the ships to the British and a letter from the German Home Office consenting to the sale. He pleaded that he had acted in good faith. The jury also acted in good faith, found him guilty, and the Judge sentenced him to 18 months in prison.[3]

Cases of trading with the enemy now came up fairly often and were reported freely in the press.

On 30 September 1914 Thomas Hartley Seed aged 54, coal merchant of Newcastle, was charged at the Newcastle Police Court with a warrant accusing him of attempting to trade with the enemy by supplying him with coal.[4] He wrote a letter dated 7 September 1914 to Carl Wohlenberg of Hamburg seeking to sell coal to Wohlenburg's company. Seed pleaded that he was acting as agent for an American shipping company and was selling coal for the use of American ships visiting Germany. He was then also charged with conspiring to defeat the rights of the Crown by the falsification of entries and the creation of false documents. Hardly surprisingly he was remanded on custody to face trial at a future date, and bail was refused. It was clear that his case was hopeless and by the time he appeared in court at Newcastle Assizes on 6 November he had changed his plea to guilty. Accordingly he was fined £100.[5]

On 9 October 1914 at Bow Street Magistrates Court Edward Wolfsohn, a teacher of languages, was charged with inciting persons to trade with the enemy. Detective Thorp of the City Police stated that he had interviewed the defendant in an hotel in Russell Square, and that he had stated that he was an American citizen. In his pocket book was a letter in German relating to the trading of apples to Germany. He was ordered to be remanded in custody to await trial. On 16 October he came before the bench again at Bow Street. It appeared that his pre-war business had been the legitimate business of accompanying schoolgirls on trips to Germany, but was also in the habit of carrying letters - some of a commercial nature. Twenty-seven such letters were found in his possession along with £70 given to him by people in Berlin. He had continued to travel back and forth to Germany during the war through neutral territory, and by carrying letters had avoided the censor, which was an offence, as well as receiving money from enemy aliens, which was another offence. He was therefore fined £3 for each letter in his possession - a total of £81.[6]

On 1 December 1914 John Frederick Drughorn was summonsed to attend at Mansion House Police Court charged with trading iron ore with the enemy.[7] The prosecution stated that he had, through an agent in Holland, sent iron ore into Germany after the outbreak of war. He had arranged terms with Swedish suppliers and the money for the ore had been sent direct to London. Drughorn's company ran a fleet of lighters up and down the Rhine from Rotterdam to the Ruhr, but because of the war the defendant took steps to continue his business through a Dutch company. Letters between Mr Drughorn and this Dutch company had been intercepted by the censor. Mr Drughorn stated that he was a Dutch citizen, but had two sons serving with the British army. Clearly having supplied his sons to the army, he saw no discrepancy in supplying the Germans the wherewithal to kill them. He was bailed at a surety of £1,000 in his own name to appear at the Central Criminal Court on 20 January 1915.

Mr Pollock, KC, submitted that iron ore was not a contraband cargo at the time of the alleged offence, that the defendant never at any point attempted to procure lighters himself to carry ore up the Rhine, but it was the Dutch who had done it. All that had happened was a perfectly lawful proceeding. The jury did not agree and found Mr Drughorn guilty. So the judge fined him one shilling, directed him to pay the costs of the prosecution, and discharged him.[8]

On 18 November 1914 a merchant named Alfred Kuppers of St Johns Wood was remanded to face trial charged with entering into new commercial and financial contracts and obligations with persons carrying on business, and residing in, Germany. He was a naturalized Briton, an American subject previously, but had been born in Germany. The two persons he was accused of trading with were British subjects who had been arrested in Frankfurt; they were in fact the defendant's brothers. Mr Kuppers was obviously a wealthy man; two people stood surety for him at £1,000 each and a further £1,000 for himself.[9]

His trial at the Old Bailey commenced on 16 January. His business was essentially a German one which traded in enamelware goods all over Europe, exporting them all over the world. Before the war much of the produce was sourced from Germany, Austria and Holland. Mr Justice Rowlatt heard the defendant plead 'not guilty' to the charges against him. Prosecuting were Mr Muir, and Mr Boyd. Defending were Mr Colam, Mr Huntley Jenkins, and Mr EJ Purchase. It is worth observing that neither the judge nor any of the Counsel were not members of the government; this is true of most of the trading with the enemy cases.

The defendant and his brothers were American citizens trading as partners. The charges related to a payment made by the defendant to a company in Holland in respect of moneys amounting to £500 due to a firm in Germany. No direct payment took place. However the jury found Mr Kuppers guilty of trading with the enemy. Mr Justice Rowlatt thought that the offence was a technical one, and especially in view of the fact that the defendant was not English - but the law had to be made to work. He sentenced Mr Kuppers to prison for one month, with leave to appeal. He could afford to appeal - his bank manager when questioned in court stated that Mr Kuppers had deposited £12,500 since the beginning of the war.[10]

Louis Bartel, shipping agent, was charged at the Guildhall Court on 16 January 1915 that he had, on 10 November 1914 attempted to enter into a commercial contract with Messrs Moeller and Schmidt of Solingen Germany for the supply of over 200 pocket knives. He had attempted to do this through an agent in neutral Holland, but the censor had intercepted his letter and sent it to the Home Office. Mr Bartel said that the letter was only an enquiry and not an order, but the Alderman magistrate, Sir John Baddeley was having none of that nonsense. He said that the matter was a small one, but it involved a great principle. He did not send Mr Bartel to a higher court but sentenced him to three months in prison.[11]

On 22 December 1914 a series of prosecutions for trading with an alien enemy came before Mr Brierley, the stipendiary magistrate at

Manchester City Police Court. Walter Isherwood was charged with actually trading with the enemy, and with deliberation, secrecy and ingenuity, attempted to develop his business interests with a company in Wurtemburg; he was the sole agent for this company in the UK which made pressed paper bobbins, and he had continued his business through an agent in Denmark. This trading with a German company was discovered by the censor who intercepted Isherwood's letters. Charges against Messrs Clifford Ltd of Fartown, Huddersfield, that they had received German bobbins from Isherwood, were reduced to one charge of receiving 500 gross. A similar charge was made against John Birch and son of Radcliffe who had also received bobbins from Isherwood. They did not deny it, but as with Cliffords, they claimed they did not know the bobbins were German. Messrs George Hattersley and Sons of Keighley made the same plea. The magistrate dismissed the charges against Cliffords and Hattersleys, but he fined Isherwood £50 and 50 guineas costs, and also fined Birch and sons £20 and costs.[12]

On 30 December 1914 Gerrit Lambertus Beukers of East Cheap was charged at the Mansion House Police Court with entering into an agreement to supply the enemy with cocoa. This generous attempt to supply the enemy with a nice bedtime drink was intercepted by the Censor on 20 October. Mr Beukers, who held a warrant to supply the Dutch Royal family with cocoa, had instructed his agents in Utrecht to supply cocoa to a merchant in Hamburg. Mr Beukers said he had not delivered a grain of cocoa to Germany since the war started and Detective Inspector MacLean, who was the investigating officer, said he had found not evidence of any deliveries being made. Mr Beukers was found guilty on the strength of his own letter, fined £100 with £50 costs - or three months in prison if he did not pay.[13]

There was no issue in England over the status of a crime of trading with the enemy. In Scotland however the matter was rather more complicated. Scots law and English law are different, though much of Scots law derives from the UK Parliament. In this case the advice from the government was that courts had to decide whether or not an incident was 'trading with the enemy', and in particular if it was a crime in Scotland.

On 4 January William Mitchell, merchant of Aberdeen, appeared before the Lord Justice General in Edinburgh, charged with trading with the enemy. Also on the bench were Lords Dundee, Salveson, Guthrie, and Hunter. This was a special case - a test case - and the opinion of the bench would be very important. The accused had entered into a contract in April 1914 to buy pickled eggs from Peter Luders, egg merchant, of Hamburg. On 23 October 1914 he wrote to Luders asking what prospects there were of getting more pickled eggs, thus attempting to obtain goods from the enemy. Luders had been supplying Russian eggs to Mitchell before the war, but now Russia was also at war with Germany.

The Solicitor General, Mr Morison, one of the government's law officers in Scotland, said that it seemed to him that the court should determine what must be the effect of the Trading with the Enemy Act.

Lord Salveson said that he would have to be satisfied that trading of any kind with an alien enemy was an offence at Common Law. Not everything contrary to law was a criminal offence. For example, if a British subject obtained rifles from the enemy he could not conceive of that as an offence. In fact, it might be a great service to the government.

The Solicitor General rejoined that the content of the letter did not matter - it was written after 4 August and was an attempt to trade and was thus an offence.

Lord Salveson came back strongly, stating that it was a monstrous thing to apprehend a man for what was not an offence at the date an act was committed; he would be very sorry to assume that such a state of affairs was meant by the legislature. However, the Bench was unanimous in their opinion that the indictment was relevant though not affecting the Common Law of Scotland. This being so, it was a crime in Scotland, if proven. The accused then pleaded not guilty and the jury was brought in.

The trial took two days and called ten witnesses. Mr Mitchell who was 77 pleaded that other suppliers in Aberdeen were able to get pickled eggs from Russia, which he had done through his German supplier, and that his customers were complaining they could not get them, so he thought he would try to satisfy them. He also said that at the time he was a 'little unhinged'.

The jury took 10 minutes to find him guilty but recommended him to mercy. The judge then sentenced him to a fine of £50 or six months in prison upon refusal to pay. The importance of the case was that it established trading with an enemy as an offence in Scottish law, and that it could be applied retrospectively.[14]

On 12 January 1915 in the High Court of Justiciary in Edinburgh Alexander Innes, tweed merchant of Hawick, was charged with conceiving a scheme for trading with the enemy through a Dutch agent in Amsterdam. He had written a letter on 8 October 1914 to his Dutch agent asking him to write to German firms and enquire if they wished any goods for summer orders. The letter was the only intelligible one that the censor had intercepted and he had certainly written it. The accused said that he had no intention of supplying the Germans during the war and that his letter had been misinterpreted. Presumably he said this because everyone expected that the war would be over by Christmas so he would indeed be able to trade with Berlin in the coming summer.

The Lord Justice General told the jury that he could see no reason why they should disbelieve the defendant. This was more or less a direction from the Bench, and they acquitted Innes very quickly.[15]

These examples demonstrate that Trading with the Enemy was a well-worn path in legal circles by mid 1915. The level of seriousness with which each case was treated depended very much on the level of offence that was alleged to have taken place. In most cases the sentences appear to have been very light and circumstances rather extenuating; there are many more such cases documented in newspapers, reported in much detail and with no apparent secrecy attached to the names of the accused, their companies, or what they were alleged to have done.

In a trial that opened in mid June in Glasgow, the names of the accused had not, until now, featured much in the press, and considering that trading with the enemy had been established as an offence in Scotland though having no effect on common law, this trial attracted a great deal of attention, a host of legal stars, a platoon of political barristers, and a lot of reporters.

A Very Liberal Trial

On Monday 14 June 1915, the train of events sparked in August 1914, by Thomas McKinnon Wood, Liberal MP and Secretary for Scotland, in initiating the search of the premises of Wm Jacks & Co came to its final act. Robert Hetherington of Newlands, Glasgow, and Henry Arnold Wilson, of Milngavie, partners in Jacks & Co came up for trial in the High Court of Justiciary in Edinburgh before the Lord Justice General of Scotland, Lord Strathclyde, the most senior judge north of Hadrian's Wall.

Until a few days before, there had been four accused, but now two of them were witnesses.

Until his elevation to the peerage in 1914 Lord Strathclyde had been plain Mr Alexander Ure, Liberal MP for Linlithgowshire, and had served as a member of the government as Solicitor General, then Lord Advocate. He has a certain notoriety in legal history, being supposed to have misled the court in the celebrated case of Oscar Slater for murder. Slater was retried in another famous case and freed on appeal with the help of Sir Arthur Conan Doyle. Ure is supposed by some to have conspired with the Procurator Fiscal, the police and the Crown Office to prevent others being tried for the murder. His promotion from government law officer to the highest bench in Scotland demonstrates that he was high in the government's confidence.

The prosecution was initiated by the Crown Agent, who was the official in charge of the Scottish Procurator Fiscal Service. His name was William Stowell Haldane and he was the brother of RB Haldane, Liberal Cabinet member, Lord Chancellor until mid May 1915, and close friend of HH Asquith.

Prosecuting for the Crown were the Lord Advocate and the Solicitor General for Scotland. The Lord Advocate was Robert Munro, Liberal MP for Wick Burghs, appointed by Asquith in 1913. In 1916 he would become Secretary for Scotland under Lloyd George.

The Solicitor General was Thomas Brash Morison, whom Asquith had appointed also in 1913, but who would not become a Liberal MP until 1917. Both men had been in their posts as government law officers since 1913 and had just been re-appointed, by Asquith, to their posts less than a week before the trial opened, on 8 June 1915. They were assisted by the Advocate Deputy, Mr Mitchell.

With such a distinguished prosecuting team it might be said that the trial was seen as one of some significance, and it is no wonder that the court room was packed, and the trial reported almost verbatim by numerous newspapers.

The defence team was originally led by Charles Scott Dickson, Conservative MP for Glasgow Central and Dean of the Faculty of Advocates, a former law officer for the Conservative government and a very able and experienced defence barrister. Unfortunately, he had to withdraw and resign his seat as he had been informed that he was to be elevated to the bench on 1 July 1915 as Lord Justice Clerk, taking the title Lord Dickson. At this date judicial appointments were made by the Lord Chancellor, who was a member of the government appointed by the Prime Minister. The Lord Chancellor in June 1915 was Stanley Buckmaster, who until 25 May had been Liberal MP for Cambridge until elevated to this very high office by Asquith. The Prime Minister trusted Buckmaster very much and had a high opinion of his abilities in running the Press Bureau since September 1914.

Dickson's place as leader of the defence team was taken by Mr JA Clyde KC and Liberal Unionist MP for Edinburgh West. Mr Clyde was to replace Dickson as Dean of the Faculty of Advocates in July 1915 and to become a Privy Counsellor and Lord Advocate in 1916, becoming Lord Clyde in 1920. He was assisted by Mr MacRobert and Mr Lippe, two distinguished barristers.

The defence was instructed by Messrs Macpherson and Mackay, Solicitors, of 26 Queen Street, Edinburgh.

The following account may be found in various forms in a range of newspapers since it was widely reported at the time, but for the purposes of this examination it is based mostly on the very detailed reporting given by the court reporter of the Glasgow Herald. This is of particular interest, because of all the reports available, this is the one, collected over several days, that Bonar Law chose to preserve among his papers.[16]

When the accused had taken their places in the dock Mr Clyde attempted to halt the trial by entering a plea of irrelevancy as urged by Mr George Robb two weeks earlier in the Sheriff's Court at a Pleading Diet. He argued that the supplying of the ore to the German companies, and the payments from the Germans had taken place in Holland and was outside the jurisdiction of British courts. This was denied by the Lord Advocate who stated that if this were the case then companies would trade with the enemy through agents and snap their fingers at the law.

The Judge thought that business persons who were found to be supplying the enemy through agents could be indicted, and where the transactions took place was not an essential consideration. The trial could proceed. The jury was then sworn and both accused pleaded Not Guilty.

The first witness, Montague Rousseau Emanuel, assistant censor at the War Office related simply how he had found letters between Jacks & Co and their agents in Rotterdam, Van Udens, which related to trading with the enemy. He passed them to the Home Office, and from thence they went to the Procurator Fiscal in Glasgow.

John Richard Kidston Law of 7 Kelvingrove Terrace Glasgow then gave evidence. He had been a partner in Jacks & Co since 1889. They had a branch at Duisburg under the management of a German subject named Carl Peters. Through this office they supplied iron ore to Krupps of Essen and other German steel companies. As late as 18 May he had been among the accused himself, as he had been since February, but in the period immediately preceding the trial, the decision had been made not to proceed with charges against him and another director, David Mitchell.

He himself had not, he stated, much knowledge of the iron ore business, and he did not know that Van Udens were agents of Jacks & Co.

The next witness, David Mitchell, also a director of Jacks & Co made it clear that the partners did not consult with each other about their business policy. He also was not connected with iron ore, but dealt in steel. The company appears to have been composed almost of different compartments, which operated independently of each other. The acceptance of this state of affairs after some months of consideration, is why neither Law nor Mitchell were in the dock.

The first day of the trial ended with the calling of Gunner Smith of HMS Falcon who had boarded the Themis in the dark of the morning just after the start of the war. He stated that none of the papers on the ship gave any indication that the cargo was bound for Germany, and that if he had known it, then he would have stopped it. However, iron ore was not on this list of prohibited goods, so Captain Wauton, his commanding officer, had authorized a certificate of clearance, which Smith had signed although he did know that there were no iron smelters in Holland. Captain Wauton could not be asked any questions as he had since been killed in action.

On the Tuesday 15 June, the Court was crowded again an especially with many members of the Bar who were in the public seats.[17] It was George Stout's turn to give evidence, and it became very clear that he, as the charter agent for the ship, had done his utmost to halt the ship and divert it to Greenock. The reason he had tried to stop it was because Mr Wilson, one of the accused, had telephoned him and asked him to do so. Arrangements were made for the ship to dock at Greenock, and the partners were very much displeased when they heard that the ship had proceeded to

Rotterdam. In his opinion, the full responsibility for this lay with Captain Gulliksen of the Themis.

Next examined was the Chartered Accountant, Robert MacFarlane, who had examined the papers of Jacks & Co on the authority of the Secretary for Scotland. The directors of Jacks & Co had given him fullest assistance and he had found that there were contracts between them and German steelworks, to supply them with iron ore. He stated that Mr Wilson took the permit from HMS Falcon to be an authority to deliver the cargo to its destination. Mr Wilson was further of opinion that the Admiralty should have known there were no blast furnaces in Holland and that the cargo would have to be sent to its final destination in Germany. Extraordinarily, Mr MacFarlane, the chartered accountant, did not know how much money had been paid for ore already delivered; he could not say for what cargo money was received. He did know that money was received from German firms and credited to the Nova Scotia Iron Company. He did not look into the question of whether Jacks & Co received a commission on any of the contracts negotiated with the German companies:

'He could not throw any light on the question of Messrs Jacks interests in these concerns at all.'[18]

Mr MacFarlane also stated that he had seen nothing of an account between Jacks & Co and Van Udens of Rotterdam. All in all, the evidence given by this extraordinary chartered accountant empowered by the Secretary for Scotland to examine the books and papers of Jacks & Co was completely inconclusive and of no help to either defence or prosecution. There was no evidence from him that the firm had profited at all and he had completely fudged and obfuscated the issue.

The next witness, Mr AC Stern of Rotterdam gave evidence simply to state that one of the partners of Van Udens had declined to journey to Britain to give evidence because of risks to his business if he did so.

Catherine MacKenzie Fraser, typist in the employ of Jacks & Co, said that she had been employed in the firm's Duisburg office when the war started. The German companies had been very anxious to get the ore. Mr Carl Peters, who was in charge of the Duisburg Office took over the negotiations to get the ore personally. She herself had not left Germany until 21 August 1914.

The defence opened their case on Wednesday 16 June. Adolphe Kunke Hillson of 19 Blytheswood Drive, Glasgow, said he had long been familiar with the German language. The Procurator Fiscal of Glasgow had submitted to him some files with a number of letters in German. He had translated these letters and he certified that they were accurate.

Alexander Muirie of Mossend, a clerk in the employ of Jacks & Co, knew of the contracts between Jacks and three German steel companies, and they were signed by Mr Wilson. He said 12,000 tons of ore were delivered to the Germans after the war had started; the cargo of the Themis was worth about £9,000. On enquiry by the Lord Advocate Mr Muirie stated that Jacks received about £1,000 from the transaction from the Krupps. When pressed as to other payments received by Jacks & Co the witness then stated that between £15,000 and £16,000 was received in total as payment for outstanding accounts. When asked if he knew that Jacks & Co had their accounts settled in respect that the Germans received the cargo of the Themis, the witness replied 'Yes'. When shown a letter from Jacks & Co to Van Udens dated 22 August 1914 suggesting that the ore be delivered to Van Udens, who would be charged for it, and they could deliver it to the Germans, the witness said that it was written on the instructions of Mr Hetherington, one of the accused.[19]

William Paterson Scott, another chartered accountant, was of much more use than Mr MacFarlane. He was clear on his figures; the Germans had received a total of £8,900 21s 9d worth of ore from the Themis. Since the start of the war they had paid their outstanding accounts to Jacks & Co to the value of £17,262 13s 8d.

Mr Clyde then demonstrated by a series of questions to the witness that this money was paid, not for the cargo of the Themis, but in settlement of cargo delivered before the start of the war. Not only that, but that Jacks & Co had acted only as agents, that the bulk of the money was gathered for the Nova Scotia Company.

Andrew McHarg, chartered accountant of Glasgow had also examined the books of Jacks & Co and found that they held nothing but agency accounts, and that there was no account on the books for Van Udens of Rotterdam. Therefore, Van Udens were not the agents of Jacks & Co. The final invoice for the ore, he stated, was sent from Duisburg to Jacks. Messers Jacks received the money and credited it to the Nova Scotia Company; thus Jacks were nothing but agents. Considering that the arrangement that was made in the end for the Germans to pay Van Udens, who then paid Jacks, this is disingenuous.

Mr Wilson, the first of the accused, was examined next. He described Jacks & Co as being divided into seven distinct departments and they dealt with Wabana ore purely as agents. They did however hold nominal shares in the Nova Scotia Iron and Steel Company to the tune of £30,000 - one eightieth of the total value. The partners of the company did not talk to each other about the work of their respective departments, but only had very general talks. As to the Themis contract he carried it on himself with no consultation with anybody. Van Udens, he said, were not agents of Jacks & Co, but had a direct connection with the Nova Scotia Company. Van Uden's job was to transport the ore from the Dutch ports where it landed to where it was required. Van Uden's charges were to be paid by Jacks & Co, but were stated in the books of Jacks & Co as between Van Udens and the Nova Scotia Company, whose agents they were. Thus, when the iron ore arrived at Rotterdam, Jacks & Co had no more responsibility other than to invoice for it.

The reason Jacks & Co had an office in Duisburg was merely to arrange for the appropriation of the ore by the purchasers. The company had tried its best to divert the Themis but had not succeeded.

On Thursday 17 June 1915 Wilson resumed his evidence on this morning, and ultimately said that not delivering the ore would be a breach of contract, that having gone up the Rhine it was 'past praying for' and that Jacks & Co thought it might be best to try to get some of the money. The main part of his defence was that since the cargo had gone beyond redemption, up the Rhine, he thought he might as well get as much money out of the Germans as he could. Mr Wilson stated that he thought silver bullets made in Germany would be very useful. This was a reference to a speech made by Lloyd George the previous October at Queens Hall London, where he said that the British had won wars with silver bullets before now, when stressing the importance of a strong economy. Lloyd George's idea had been that the country with the most money would be the one that won, and that the outcome might come down to whoever had the last £400,000,000. The implication was that by wringing money out of Germany, Mr Wilson had done his patriotic duty. Perhaps he was joking.

Mr Clyde, the defending barrister, was also in joking mood and asked Mr Wilson his nationality, to which he confessed that he was English and had no connection with Germany; to which Mr Clyde replied 'There is only one defect - you are not a Scotsman' causing laughter in the court and the witness to smile. In explanation of the warm tone of his letters to the Germans he explained that they were old business friends and it never struck him that using the word 'friends' was done by him in any but the ordinary way. The Germans had stuck to their contracts and paid what was due. Since the greater part of the cargo had already gone to Germany before Jacks & Co was aware of it, they consented the rest should follow. This succeeded in getting the £16,000 for the Nova Scotia Company which was then credited with that amount. There was a much larger amount, some £19,000 - £20,000 which was due from German companies to the Nova Scotia Company for previous Themis deliveries, but he could not see how that would be paid before then end of the war.

The Court adjourned for lunch, after which the other accused, Robert Hetherington, was called to take the stand.

Mr Hetherington looked after the Wabana ore for Jacks & Co, but had no conversation with Mr Wilson about it until Wilson had gone on holiday on 14 August; then they discussed the position. To his mind the ore was at Rotterdam and beyond their control. At the same time he wished to do everything he could to hold it back until they could get payment for it. He had not in his mind that he was trading with the enemy; he never had any other idea otherwise than acting loyally and honourably. When pressed on the question of whether or not what he did was against the national interest the witness gave his opinion that it would be. He knew that it was his duty to take every possible means to prevent the Germans from getting the ore, but the ore was under the control of Van Udens. When asked if he had instructed Van Udens to deliver the ore, he stated that they had agreed to Van Udens's proposals. Asked if he knew it was his duty to prevent the delivery he asserted that he did not think he had any right to prevent it.

That concluded the evidence; the accused had to wait until the following day to hear the verdict.

On Friday morning, 18 June, the court was again packed. There were three counts to the charges relating to supplying or consenting to supply the enemy with goods, and two that they did in fact supply goods to Krupps and two other German companies. By a majority, the jury returned verdicts of guilty, but with a unanimous recommendation to mercy on account of the unprecedented circumstances of the case.

The Lord Advocate, speaking for the Crown, asked the jury to find the men guilty of what he called a grave and deplorable crime. They were not dealing with ignorant or unlettered men, but men of considerable standing, men of mental calibre, men of ripe business experience, responsible men of the world and affairs.

He argued that Jacks & Co had as much control over the iron ore at Rotterdam as they would have had if it had been at Glasgow Docks. They made no attempt to prevent it from going to the Germans, and only prohibited Van Udens from handing it over to the Germans without payment. Terms having been settled, they arranged to give the ore - and gave it. Van Udens acted as agents for Jacks & Co throughout. The Germans got the ore and Jacks & Co got the cash.

The excuse that the Admirality had let the ore pass was a flimsy one; it was their duty to stop the ship, and he conceded that up to 12 August their conduct had been as faultless as Adam and Eve in the garden of Eden, but after that date the serpent had entered the garden when the first suggestion was made of what prospect of payment there was if the goods went to Germany. *The Times*, next day, remarked that this statement made it very clear that the Lord Advocate was very aware of human frailty in the matter of profit

Mr Clyde, in making his statement for the defence contended that his clients had concocted no scheme, no deception, any concealment or hidden any interest, and that Jacks & Co had recognized that from the first moment that war was declared there would be no further shipments of ore to Germany. What the defendants had done had arisen out of an unpremeditated and unprecedented circumstance. In this respect they did nothing indictable until 18 September 1914, and then by an alteration to law which had taken place on 27 November. They may have made mistakes, but they were not crimes until made so retrospectively.

Mr Clyde further contended that once the cargo reached Van Udens, it was then, by transfer of the bills of lading, the property of the Germans, and that Jacks & Co could not have supplied goods that were already the Germans' property. In his opinion, that knocked the bottom out of the indictment.

He went further - that there was no illegality or criminality attached even now to the getting of money from a German. All the defendants wanted was payment of debts already due; they had in fact obstructed to their best ability the passage of the ore upriver, when the ore was already the German's property. How could this support a charge of supplying the enemy with goods?

The Lord Justice General took 55 minutes to sum up what he described as a grave and important case, yet he did not believe that the jury would find that it was attended with any real difficulty because there was no conflict of evidence.

At 11 o'clock on 4 August 1914 it became a criminal act for any resident of this country to have financial or commercial relations with any person resident in Germany. Nothing short of a Royal license would allow such a transaction.

The only direction that Jacks & Co could have given that was a crime was to deliver the ore to the three German firms. They might have given any direction they pleased or said that it was no business of theirs. The only defence they might have given is that they were compelled to deliver the ore, but that was no answer to the indictment; they had not been compelled.

It was quite clear that the Lord Justice General took the view that the defendants had acquiesced in the delivery of the ore in exchange for the settling of their accounts.

The Jury still took 75 minutes to consider their verdict because they could not agree. By a majority, they found the defendants guilty, and they desired unanimously to submit to the court that the utmost possible leniency be exercised in favour of the accused.

His Lordship then addressed the accused, saying that they had been convicted of a series of charges, the gravity of which they were fully conversant with. The crime was one that warranted a long period of penal servitude in addition to a fine, but he had given full consideration to the recommendation that the jury had thought fit to make. He sentenced them to imprisonment for six months, each of them to pay a fine of £2,000, and in default of payment, to serve a further six months in jail.

An extraordinary trial with a galaxy of legal luminaries was at an end; the matter of Wm Jacks & Co trading with the enemy could hardly have been in safer hands if someone had handpicked the judge and counsel on both sides. Two rogue traders had overstepped the mark and they paid the penalty, though when their sentences were over, both men went back to work for Jacks & Co. Jack Law had not a stain on his character, and his brother, the leader of the Conservative Party, and His Majesty's Secretary for the Colonies, who had thousands of pounds on deposit at interest in Jacks & Co, was free from all blemish too.

There had been a number of cases tried since the start of the war where companies had been found guilty of trading with the enemy. Some of them had been tried in Police Courts, others in Assizes, but this one, in front of the highest judge in the land, with so many notable members of parliament involved, was in a different league altogether; a special case, quite clearly. Justice had been seen to be done.

Themis, the goddess of Justice, contrary to myth, is not blind. She wears a blindfold, and when she wishes, she sees clearly enough. On Friday 18 June 1915 she might also have been seen to laugh.

The New York Times of 19 June did not imply political interference with the case but thought the sentences 'amazingly light' and pointed out that many other companies had goods in Rotterdam at the very outset of war that were bound for Germany, and they cancelled deliveries without difficulty. The newspaper did not take the fines seriously, pointing out that individuals seldom paid such fines.

On the day that the verdict was announced it was Bonar Law's friend Max Aitken, later Lord Beaverbrook, who received the news and went to find him to tell him. He found him, as he knew he would, at the Baldwin Club, 3 Pall Mall East, playing bridge, which he was fond of doing. Aitken persuaded Bonar Law with difficulty to leave the table to talk of personal matters and eventually drew him aside. On hearing of the verdict Bonar Law became deeply distressed and broke into tears. The two accused just found guilty were old friends of his, of many years standing and he felt they had been hardly treated; he was lucky in that his brother had not also been in the dock, as he might well have been until charges were dropped a few days before the trial. Quite obviously the Conservative leader had been under a considerable strain and it is very likely that some of his tears were of pure relief at his own release from unbearable strain. [20]

The relief within the rest of the Law family must have been palpable, but the ordeal was not quite over.

Conclusion

On Thursday 24 June Bonar Law came to see Asquith as Margot related, because Asquith was about to be asked a question in the House:

'...*very* unhappy over that maniac Ginnell who is going to ask me in the House today what Bonar's relations are, or have been to the firm of Jacks that have just been convicted and punished for selling munitions to Germany. Bonar's brother is in the firm and it's altogether a very nasty affair. Poor devil, he was ready to give up leading the Opposition, in fact chuck *everything.* I told him not to be a fool. I can't imagine a more idiotic thing to do! I would be sorrier for him, but I can't help thinking after the way he behaved- believing every low rumour about our men.... That this is retribution, '[21]

To add to the weight on Bonar Law's mind must have been the very personal upset and grief caused by the news, received less than two weeks before this, that his 19 year old nephew, John Robley, who had quit his job at Jacks & Co the previous year to join the navy, had been killed at the Dardanelles. To judge by the events of the following day Asquith clearly advised Bonar Law to head the question off by answering it himself. To judge by the reaction of members after Bonar Law spoke, it is probable that this was not all that Asquith did.

As it was, when Bonar Law was asked about his connection with Jacks & Co, after the trial and in late June, his answer might be seen as a little economical with the truth, considering the amounts he had placed with the company. Since he was being paid a fixed rate of interest, the only place that could have come from would be company profits:

'STATEMENT BY MR. BONAR LAW.

Mr. GINNELL asked the Prime Minister whether any Member of His Majesty's Government holds, or held until recently, a financial interest in the firm of Jacks & Company, recently convicted of trading with the enemy?

The SECRETARY of STATE for the COLONIES (Mr. Bonar Law) As this question refers to me, perhaps I may be permitted to answer it myself. I was for many years a member of the firm referred to in the question, and I was still a partner in it when I entered the House of Commons in 1900. For some months afterwards I continued my connection with it, but I came to the conclusion that I had to choose between business and politics, and at the end of the year 1901 I gave up my business, and I gave it up absolutely. Since then—that is for more than thirteen years—I have had no control over the business. I have had no knowledge of the way in which it was conducted, and, although I have from time to time put money on deposit with them at a fixed rate of interest, I have had no share, direct or indirect, in the profits or losses of the firm. [22]

Mr Laurence Ginnell was the Irish Nationalist member for Westmeath and was clearly bent on more than a mild mischief. Immediately Bonar Law had finished, Sir Arthur Markham leaped to Bonar Law's defence and asked if there might be an enquiry into the mind of the member who asked such questions in the House? Markham was a Liberal; and Asquith had been forewarned of Ginnell's question.

The Liberal Party, who owed Bonar Law a lot of payback for a lot of abuse and innuendo on a large number of matters, stayed silent in a startling and disciplined way; nobody said a word about the Jacks affair, though Bonar Law's head could have been on a plate for the asking. It is a singular fact that this was the only statement that Bonar Law was ever required to make on his connection with the company.

On 25 June HA Gwynne thundered with great guns against Mr Ginnell:

'No-one but the parliamentary pariah who sits for North Westmeath would have dreamed of asking a question of the kind. Whatever may be thought of his political views or his political talents there is no man in the House whose personal reputation is higher than that of Mr Bonar Law.' [23]

That was emphatically that; ranks had been closed across the parties to stifle any threat to Bonar Law. A more complete contrast between this and the extensive rows on the Marconi share dealing of Lloyd George and Rufus Isaacs in 1913 could scarce be found. In the absence of party rivalry the Jacks case was a prime opportunity for Liberal back benchers to exact revenge on the Conservatives for their attempts to force Lloyd George's resignation the year before. Despite a coalition just having been formed, the only explanation for the absolute quiet on the Liberal benches must be that party discipline was in full force; they had been told to be quiet. Bonar Law got off very lightly indeed with only the lively Mr Ginnell to defy the resolute and apparent determination of the rest of the House to say nothing and hush things up.

In the loom of time where the cloth of history is woven, the pattern that emerges depends very much on the threads that are chosen. In the broadness of this particular cloth are stripes of compulsion, shortage of shells, resignation of a Sea Lord, coalition and the marriage of a Prime Minister's muse. To which must be added the effect of the Jacks trial upon a Conservative leader, against a lurid background of hysterical anti-Germanism, rumours of plots, the sinking of an ocean liner, and Zeppelin raids on Britain.

It is a version of truth, and perhaps no more valid than others, and the whole of it may never be known, simply because the design of the main protagonist was that it never should be known; a man who admitted that he took delight at the thought of the frustration in future biographers. Yet he left one clue to anyone in the future who might think they knew his mind, and it is perhaps the most fitting note upon which to end. He was apparently completely and utterly indifferent to what History might say of him.

In March 1915 Asquith wrote a piece of whimsy - or what appears to be whimsy - to Venetia Stanley, describing what may, or may not be himself appearing in front of Rhadamanthus, judge of the dead, who opens an address to him, The Shade, thus:

Rhadamanthus; "You were, in the world above, a classic example of Luck. You were endowed at birth with brains above the average. You had, further, some qualities of temperament which are exceptionally useful for mundane success- energy under the guise of lethargy, a faculty for working quickly, which is more effective in the long run than plodding perseverance; patience (which is one of the rarest of human qualities); a temperate but persistent ambition; a clear mind, a certain facility and lucidity of speech; intellectual but not moral, irritability; a natural tendency to understand and appreciate the opponent's point of view; and as time went on and your nature matured, a growing sense of proportion, which had its effect upon friends and foes, and which, coupled with detachment from any temptation to intrigue, and in regard to material interests and profits, an unaffected indifference, secured for you the substantial advantage of personality and authority.

"The really great men of the world are the geniuses and saints. You belonged to neither category. Your intellectual equipment (well cultivated and trained) still left you far short of the one; your spiritual limitations and

your endowment of 'The Old Adam" left you still shorter of the other…

"You had excellent health, a good digestion, an adequate capacity for sleep, unabated authority in your Cabinet, big events to confront and provide for…"

<u>The Shade;</u> *"Not Bad! I could have made the same speech without preparation in the House of Commons. Its only defect is that it ignores the central reality of my life."*

<u>Rhadamanthus;</u> *"What was that?"*

<u>The Shade;</u> *"It is something beyond the ken of your damned tribunal. Give me my sentence and call up the next ghost".[24]*

Asquith then, may not be known, nor read like a book. By his own admission he was lucky; but it could equally be said that his Cabinet was also lucky because in him they found a builder of bridges, and to judge by their performances with each other, it is doubtful that anyone else was around who could have held them together in the way that he did. It could not be claimed that Asquith was a great war leader during this period by any means, but he went on to be Prime Minister for more than half the first world war, and the things which ultimately won that war were conceived on his watch.

It is safe to say that in a period in which Britain faced things she had never before faced in her history, by trial and error, by mistakes and blunders, by triumphs and defeats she began to see the way to achieve a victory in a war that she had never wanted. The man at the helm during this time, whoever it was, would also have made mistakes; would also have had to bear in mind the same considerations of labour, politics, personalities, diplomacy and so on, that Asquith did. He was a competent leader at this time of trial - and probably more competent than most.

Epilogue

In December 1916 the Themis left the Tyne heading for the Netherlands. On or about 21 December she hit a mine in the North Sea and sank; all 19 men on board died. It is possible that she hit a drifting mine that had broken loose- British mines were notorious for doing this, or that she strayed out of the passages marked through the thick North Sea minefields. At any rate, the ship which may have put such pressure on the Conservative leader that he almost resigned, was no more.

A glance at diving websites will reveal that the Themis is a site for divers. One of them commented in 2009:

'Dived this wreck in June 2009. Nice dive, superstructure still intact. Found 2 guns. One at the fore part and one just after the bridge. Must have been an armed cargo, certainly not a destroyer. The gun at the front lies in a strange position: when you are at the end of the front part, the gun lies some metres before it in the sand, pointing downwards. It looks as if a big part of the bow has disappeared in the sand.'

Guns?

Even in death, the Themis provides mystery.

Endnotes

Chapter 1

1 Glasgow Herald Tuesday 15 June 1915. Bonar Law Papers. Parliamentary Archives BL64/D/4

2 http://www.wrecksite.eu/wreck.aspx?9776

3 Churchill W (1929) *The World Crisis* Odhams Press pp. 154-155

4 Webb. M (2014) *from Downing Street to the Trenches.* Bodleian Library, Oxford p. 33

5 Riddell. Lord (1933) *Lord Riddell's War Diary.* Ivor Nicholson & Watson p. 3

6 Bonar Law to Asquith 2 August 1914. Bonar Law Papers. Parliamentary Archives BL/37/4/1

7 CP Scott to J Dillon 9 August in Wilson T (1970) *The Political Diaries of CP Scott 1911-1928.* Collins p, 100

8 Churchill ibid. p. 191

9 Brock M & E (1982) *HH Asquith. Letters to Venetia Stanley.* Oxford Press P. 299

10 Beaverbrook undated notes. Beaverbrook Papers. Parliamentary Archives. G5 vi

11 de Courcy A (2014) *Margot at War. Love and Betrayal in Downing Street 1912-1916. Weidenfield & Nicolson. Kindle ed. Loc 2471*

12 Brock M & E ibid p. 529

13 Hazlehurst C. (1971) *Politicians at War* Jonathan Cape p. 301

14 David. E (ed) (1977) *From the Diaries of Charles Hobhouse* John Murray p. 184

15 Webb M ibid p47

16 LS Amory to Bonar Law 26 August 1914. Bonar Law Papers. Parliamentary Archives. BL/37/4/1

17 Robert Williams to Ramsay McDonald cited in French D (1982) *British Economic and Strategic Planning, 1905-1915* Allen & Unwin p. 191.

18 Minutes of the PRC. British Library *Add Mss. 54192A*

Chapter 2

[1] Edinburgh Evening News - Tuesday 15 June 1915
Image © Johnston Press plc. Image created courtesy of THE BRITISH LIBRARY BOARD.

[2] Daily Record - Tuesday 15 June 1915
Image © Trinity Mirror. Image created courtesy of THE BRITISH LIBRARY BOARD.

[3] Coventry Evening Telegraph - Tuesday 15 June 1915
Image © Trinity Mirror. Image created courtesy of THE BRITISH LIBRARY BOARD.

[4] Dundee Evening Telegraph - Tuesday 15 June 1915
Image © D.C.Thomson & Co. Ltd. Image created courtesy of THE BRITISH LIBRARY BOARD.

[5] Asquith to Bonar Law 8 August 1914 Bonar Law Papers. Parliamentary Archives *BL 34/3/20*

[6] George V to Asquith 25 August 1914 Asquith Papers. Bodleian Library. *F4.*

[7] CP Scott Diary entry 3 August 1914 in Wilson T (1970) *The Political Diaries of CP Scott 1911-1928.* Collins p. 100

[8] ibid p100

[9] James Hope to Lord Edmund Talbot 1 September 1914. Bonar Law Papers. Parliamentary Archives BL34/5/6

[10] John W Hills to Bonar Law 6 September 1914 Bonar Law Papers Parliamentary Archives BL34/5/20

[11] Hazlehurst C (1971) *Politicians at War July 1914 to May 1915* Jonathan Cape.p. 158)

[12] Brock M & E (1982) *HH Asquith. Letters to Venetia Stanley.* Oxford Press p. 315

[13] Mosley L (1961) *Curzon; the end of an epoch.* Longmans Green & Co. pp. 154-5)

[14] John Baird to Bonar Law 19 September 1914. Bonar Law Papers Parliamentary Archives BL 34/6/59

[15] Brock M & E (1982) *HH Asquith. Letters to Venetia Stanley.* Oxford Press p. 343

[16] ibid p. 395

[17] Austen Chamberlain to Lloyd George 18 November 1914 Lloyd George Papers Parliamentary Archives. C/3/14/6

[18] Beaverbrook Lord (1960) *Politicians and the War 1914-1916.* Oldbourne p. 33

[19] Zebel S (1973) *Balfour* Cambridge University Press p.199)

[20] Long to Bonar Law 25 November 1914 Long Papers. British Library add. Mss. 62404).

[21] Cassar. G (1994) *Asquith as War Leader* Hambledon Press p.31

[22] 288

[23] Walter Long. *Hansard.* HC Deb 12 November 1914 vol 68 cc43-166

[24] Brock M&E ibid p. 315

[25] Stubbs J. (1975) Impact of the Great War on the Conservatives. In Peele G & Cook C. *The Politics of Reappraisal 1918-1939. Palgrave MacMillan p. 22*

[26] Koss. S (1969) *Lord Haldane- scapegoat for Liberalism* Columbia University Press.

[27] Koss S (1976) *Asquith* Allen Lane p. 167

[28] Brock M & E (2014) *Margot Asquith's Great War Diary 1914-1916.* Oxford University Press. Kindle ed. Loc 4018

Chapter 3

[29] Dundee Evening Telegraph - Tuesday 15 June 1915
Image © D.C.Thomson & Co. Ltd. Image created courtesy of THE BRITISH LIBRARY BOARD.

[30] Birmingham Gazette - Wednesday 16 June 1915
Image © Trinity Mirror. Image created courtesy of THE BRITISH LIBRARY BOARD.

[31] Glasgow Herald Tuesday 15 June 1915. Bonar Law Papers. Parliamentary Archives BL64/D/4

32 loc cit.

33 Douglas R. (1970)   <u>Voluntary Enlistment in the First world war and the work of the Parliamentary Recruiting Committee.</u> *Journal of Modern History* 42(4)1 pp. 564-585

34 op cit p. 577

35 Robert Cecil. Undated notes end 1914. Cecil Papers. British Library Add. Mss. *51195*

36 Hugh Cecil to Bonar Law 9 November 1914. Bonar Law Papers. Parliamentary Archives. BL35/2/18.

37 Long to Bonar Law 25 November 1914. Long Papers. British Library. Add. Mss. 62404

38 Long to Gwynne December 1914 Gwynne Papers. Cited in Grieves. K. (1988) *The Politics of Manpower 1914-18.* Manchester University Pres. P. 14

39 Boraston to Bonar Law 9 November 1914. Bonar Law Papers. Parliamentary Archives. BL 35/2/16

40 HC Deb 08 February 1915 vol 69 cc277-382

41 Asquith to George V. 16 December 1914. National Archives PRO CAB22/1

42 Wrench JE. (1955) *Geoffrey Dawson and Our Times.* Hutchinson p.115

43 Holmes R (2004) *Tommy* Harper Perrenial p 139

44 Dundee Courier Wed 16 June 1915 British Library Newspaper Archive

45 HC Deb 25 November 1914 vol 68 cc1224-7

46 Brock M & E (1982) *HH Asquith. Letters to Venetia Stanley.* Oxford Press p. 329

47 Walter Long to Col Repington Jan 1 1915.' Long Papers. British Library. Add.Mss. 62419

48 Long to Bonar Law 4 January 1915 Bonar Law Papers. Parliamentary Archives BL 36/1/4

49 HL Deb 06 January 1915 vol 18 cc231-62

50 HL Deb 08 January 1915 vol 18 cc347-408

51 HL Deb 08 January 1915 vol 18 cc347-408

[52] Brock M & E op cit p. 371

[53] op cit. p. 372

[54]Lansdowne to Bonar Law 10 January 1915. Bonar Law Papers. Parliamentary Archives. L BL 36/1/12

[55] Hazlehurst C (1971) *Politicians at War July 1914 to May 1915* Jonathan Cape.p.158)

[56] Pugh M (1974) Asquith, Bonar Law and the First Coalition. *The Historical Journal xvii, 4 pp 813-836*

[57] Crewe to Bonar Law 11 January 1915. Bonar Law Papers. Parliamentary Archives BL 36/1/14

[58] Zebel S (1973) *Balfour* Cambridge University Press p. 202

Chapter 4

[1] Brock M & E (1982) *HH Asquith. Letters to Venetia Stanley.* Oxford Press p. 258

[2] Asquith to George V 13 January 1915 Asquith Papers. Bodleian Library Asq 8

[3] Diary of John Burns 22 January 1915 British Library Add. MSS. 46337

[4] Professor AF Pollard letter to *The Times* 22 January 1915

[5] Mr Edward Goulding MP to Bonar Law   16 January 1915 Bonar Law Papers. Parliamentary Archives BL36/1/25

[6] Brock M & E (2014) *Margot Asquith's Great War Diary 1914-1916.* Oxford University Press.

[7] Curzon to Long 24 January 1915. Long Papers. British Library Add. Mss. 62419

[8] Curzon Memorandum to Shadow Cabinet colleagues 24 Jan 1915 Bonar Law Papers Parliamentary Archives BL 36/2/46

[9] Long to Shadow Cabinet colleagues 27 January 1915 Long Papers. British Library Add. Mss. 62419

[10] Stubbs. J (1975) in Peele G & Cook C (eds) *The Politics of Reappraisal 1918-1939.* MacMillan pp. 14-38

[11] Hazlehurst C (1971) *Politicians at War July 1914 to May 1915* Jonathan Cape. P. 199

[12] Middlemass K & Barnes J (1969) *Baldwin* Weidenfeld & Nicolson p. 57

[13] Walter Long Memorandum to Shadow Cabinet Colleagues 27 January 1915. Long Papers. British Library Add. Mss. *62419*

[14] Lansdowne to Long 28 January 1915. Long Papers. British Library Add. Mss. 62403

[15] loc cit.

[16] Lansdowne to Bonar Law 28 January 1915 Lansdowne Papers. British Library 5/88/ 38

[17] Bonar Law to Lansdowne, copied to Long, 29 January 1915. Long Papers. British Library Add. Mss. 62419 and Lansdowne Papers 88/39

[18] Lord Methuen letter to *The Times*. Lansdowne Papers. British Library. Lansdowne c9-4 p. 6-2

[19] Lord Methuen to Lansdowne 29 January 1915 Lansdowne Papers. British Library Lansdowne c9-5 p6-3 01-4

[20] Curzon's memorandum to Shadow Cabinet colleagues January 1915. Bonar Law Papers. Parliamentary Archives BL 36/2/46

[21] *Bonar Law to Lansdowne 29 January 1915 Bonar Law Papers. Parliamentary Archives. BL 88/39 and British Library Lansdowne Papers C10*

[22] Gilbert. B (1992) *David Lloyd George*. Batsford. P. 181

[23] Stubbs. Op cit. p24

[24] Adams RJQ. (1999) *Bonar Law* John Murray p. 176

[25] *The Times* 18 November 1931

[26] Long to Bonar Law 2 February 1915. Bonar Law Papers. Parliamentary Archives BL *36/2/46*

[27] Sir George Goldie to Lord Lansdowne 6 Feb 1916. Lansdowne Papers British Library uncatalogued Lansdowne Papers.

[28] HC Deb 09 February 1915 vol 69 cc408-540

[29] Lloyd George Memorandum to Cabinet 22 February 1915. National Archives Cab 24/1

[30] John Burns Diary 5 February 1915. Burns Papers. British Library Add. Mss. 46337

[31] *Report on the state of employment in the UK Feb 1915. Parliamentary Accounts and Papers XXVIII cd 7939.*

[32] *Kitchener memorandum to Cabinet 25 February 1915 on conduct of war. National Archives. CAB 24/1*

[33] Lord Willoughby de Broke to Lansdowne 23 Feb 1914 Lansdowne papers British Library. Uncatalogued Lansdowne Papers.

[34] Brock M & E (1982) *HH Asquith. Letters to Venetia Stanley.* Oxford Press p 432

[35] A Rowntree to Mary Rowntree 16 February 1915 in Packer E. (ed) (2002) *The letters of Arnold Stephenson Rowntree to Mary Katherine Rowntree 1910-1918.* Cambridge University Press p. 178

[36] Exeter and Plymouth Gazette - Tuesday 23 February 1915 Image © Local World Limited. Image created courtesy of THE BRITISH LIBRARY BOARD.

[37] Bonar Law to Max Aitken 19 Mar 1915 Beaverbrook Papers. Parliamentary Archives. Beaverbrook C202

Chapter 5

[1] Asquith to Lansdowne 8 March 1915 Lansdowne Papers British Library uncatalogued Lansdowne Papers 103.

[2] Bonar L to Asquith 8 March 1915. Bonar Law Papers Parliamentary Archives *BL36/6/1*

[3] Brock M & E. (1982) *HH Asquith. Letters to Venetia Stanley.* Oxford Press p. 480

[4] Churchill W (1927) *The World Crisis 1911-1918* Odhams Press p. 798

[5] Webb M. (ed) (2014) *From Downing Street to the Trenches.* Bodleian Press Oxford p.92

[6] Roskill S. (1970) *Hankey Man of Secrets Vol 1 1877-1918* Collins p159

[7] Brock M&E. op cit. p. 469)

[8] Roskill S. op cit p. 161

[9] HC Deb 11 March 1915 vol 70 cc1571-601

[10] HC Deb 11 March 1915 vol 70 cc1571-601

[11] Gibson Bowles to Long 12 March 1915. Long Papers. British Library Add. Mss. 62419

[12] Gwynne to Bonar Law 26 March 1915. Bonar Law Papers. Parliamentary Archives BL 36/6/36)

[13] Loc Cit.

[14] Loc Cit.

[15] de Courcy A. (2014) *Margot at War: Love and Betrayal in Downing Street 1912-16 Weidenfeld & Nicolson. Kindle ed.* loc 4356)

[16] Brock M&E. op cit. p. 495

[17] Koss S (1976) *Asquith.* Allen Lane p. 180

[18] Brock M&E. op cit. p. 505

[19] Edward D. (1977) *Inside Asquith's Cabinet* John Murray p. 233

[20] Op cit. p. 233

[21] Riddell Lord (1933) *Lord Riddell's War Diary* Ivor Nicolson & Watson p. 68)

[22] Edward D. op cit. p. 238

[23] Brock M&E. op cit. p. 524

[24] Lord Scarborough to Lord Lansdowne 20 March 1915. Lansdowne Papers. British Library uncatalogued Lansdowne Papers 88/46

[25] Lord Scarborough to Sir George Goldie 25 March 1915. Loc cit.

[26] Sir George Goldie to Lord Lansdowne 21 March 1915 Loc cit.

[27] Lord Hardinge Memorandum to Kitchener 1 Feb 1915. Kitchener papers. National Archives. PRO 30/57/69)

[28] Wilson T (1966) *The Downfall of the Liberal Party 1914-1935.* Collins p. 59

[29] Lord Lansdowne to Sir George Goldie 23 March 1915. Loc Cit.

[30] Lord Lansdowne to Bonar Law 3 April 1915 Loc cit. 88/41

[31] Asquith to George V 8 April 1915. National Archives. CAB37/127/14

[32] John Burns' Diary 28 March 1915 Burns Papers. British Library. Add. Mss. 46337

[33] Koss. S. op cit. p.180

[34] GH Robb to Bonar Law April 1915. Bonar Law Papers. Parliamentary Archives. BL37/3/14

Chapter 6

[1] Brock M & E. (1982) *HH Asquith. Letters to Venetia Stanley.* Oxford Press p. 527

[2] Edward D. (1977) *Inside Asquith's Cabinet* John Murray p. 235

[3] Blake R (1955) *The Unknown Prime Minister* Eyre & Spottiswoode p. 239

[4] Adams RJQ. (1999) *Bonar Law* John Murray p. 179

[5] Brock M & E. op cit. p. 541

[6] Riddell Lord (1933) *Lord Riddell's War Diary* Ivor Nicolson & Watson p. 73

[7] Gilbert B. (1992) *David Lloyd George* Batsford. p. 166

[8] Brock M & E. op cit. p. 545

[9] Hankey M (1961) *The Supreme Command 1914-1918* George Allen & Unwin P. 311

[10] Brock M & E (2014) *Margot Asquith's Great War Diary 1914-1916.* Oxford University Press. Kindle Ed. P. CXIVIII

[11] Brock M & E. (1982) *HH Asquith. Letters to Venetia Stanley.* Oxford Press p. 552

[12] Asquith HH (1919) *The Great Shell Story; Mr Asquith's reply to Lord French* Cassell & Co. p. 41

[13] Brock M & E. op cit. p. 559

[14] Sandhurst Viscount. (1928) *From day to day 1914-1915* Edward Arnold. P. 179

[15] Riddell Lord. Op cit. p. 81

[16] Asquith to George V 8 April 1915 National Archives. CAB 37/127/14

[17] Bonar Law to Lansdowne 13 April 1915.Lansdowne Papers. British Library uncatalogued Lansdowne Papers

[18] Brock M & E (2014) *Margot Asquith's Great War Diary 1914-1916.* Oxford University Press. Kindle Ed. P. CXIVIII

[19] Riddell Lord. Op cit. p. 80

[20] Brock M & E. op cit. p. 568

[21] HC Deb 21 April 1915 vol 71 cc277-374

[22] Grieves. K. (1988) *The Politics of Manpower 1914-18.* Manchester University Press. P. 14

[23] HC Deb 21 April 1915 vol 71 cc277-374

[24] Loc cit.

[25] HC Deb 04 May 1915 vol 71 cc960-1

[26] Wilson K. (ed) (1988) *The Rasp of War* Sidgewick & Jackson p. 86

[27] Beaverbrook Lord (19600 2nd ed.) *Politicians and the war 1914- 1916.* Oldbourne p. 88

[28] Fraser P (1982) Lord Beaverbrook's fabrications in *Politicians and the War 1914-1916.* The Historical Journal, 25, 1 pp147-166

[29] Lord Northcliffe to Sir John French 1 May 1915. Northcliffe Papers. British Library . Add. Mss. 62159

[30] Sandhurst Viscount. Op cit. p. 188

[31] Asquith to Sir John French 9 January 1915. Asquith Papers. Bodleian Library Asq. 26/206

[32] French to Kitchener 30 August 1914. Bonar Law Papers Parliamentary Archives   BL/56/xi/4

[33] Holmes R (1981) *The little Field Marshal* Jonathon Cape.

[34] Strachan. H (2003) *The First World War* Simon & Schuster. P176

[35] Ballard CR. (1930) *Kitchener* Newnes p. 256

[36] Riddell Lord. Op cit. p. 97

[37] John Burns' diary 3 May 1915. Burns Papers. British Library Add. Mss. 46337

[38] Wilson T (ed) (1970) *The Political Diaries of CP Scott* Collins. P138

[39] Lord Northcliffe to HG Wells 8 May 1915 Northcliffe Papers. British Library. Add. Mss. 62121

[40] Gilbert B op cit p. 190

[41] Hewins Diary 6 May 1915. Cited in Stubbs J (1975) The politics of Reappraisal 1918-1939 in Peele G & Cook C (eds) *The Politics of Reappraisal 1918-1939.* MacMillan p. 26

[42] Cutting from *Justice* 6 May 1915 Bonar Law Papers. Parliamentary Archives. BL/64/D2

[43] Loc Cit. BL/64/D/3

[44] Loc cit.

[45] Loc cit. BL/64/D6

[46] Birmingham Gazette 14 May 1915 British Library Newspaper Archives. Image © Trinity Mirror. Image created courtesy of THE BRITISH LIBRARY BOARD.

[47] Sheffield evening Telegraph 14 May 1915 loc cit. Image © Johnston Press plc. Image created courtesy of THE BRITISH LIBRARY BOARD.

[48] Taunton Courier and Advertiser 12 May 1915 loc cit. Image © Local World Limited. Image created courtesy of THE BRITISH LIBRARY BOARD.

[49] HC Deb 13 May 1915 vol 71 cc1841-78

[50] Birmingham Daily Mail 17 May 1915 loc. Cit. Image © Trinity Mirror. Image created courtesy of THE BRITISH LIBRARY BOARD.

[51] Gilbert. B op cit. p. 168

[52] HC Deb 04 May 1915 vol 71 cc1018-79

[53] loc cit.

[54] Stubbs J (1975) The politics of Reappraisal 1918-1939 in Peele G & Cook C (eds) *The Politics of Reappraisal 1918-1939.* MacMillan p. 26

[55] Pugh M (1974) Asquith, Bonar Law and the First Coalition. The Historical Journal XVII, 4 p. 825

Chapter 7

[1] Long to Bonar Law 12 May 1915. Bonar Law Papers. Parliamentary Archives. BL 27/2/19

[2] HC Deb 12 May 1915 vol 71 c1642

[3] John Burns' Diary 13 May 1915. Burns Papers. British Library. Add. Mss. 46337

[4] Brock M & E. (2014) *Margot Asquith's Great War Diary 1914-1916* Oxford University Press. Kindle ed. P. CXIVIII

[5] loc cit

[6] Lloyd George 17 August 1910 Document on Coalition. Bonar Law Papers. British Library. BL C/3/14/8

[7] Wilson K. (ed) (1988) *The Rasp of War* Sidgewick & Jackson p. 87

[8] ibid p. 89

[9] loc.cit

[10] Adams RJQ (1999) *Bonar Law.* John Murray p. 182

[11] Bonar Law to Long 14 May 1915. Long Papers. British Library Add. Mss. 62404

[12] Koss. S (1976) *Asquith* Allen Lane p . 184

[13] ibid p. 185

[14] Beaverbrook Lord (1960)*Politicians and the War 1914-1916.* Oldbourne Book Co. ltd. P. 51

[15] Long to Bonar Law 16 May 1915. Bonar Law Papers. British Library. BL/49/1/3

[16] Long to Bonar Law 16 May 1915. Bonar Law Papers. British Library BL37/2/324

[17] Wilson K (ed) (1988) *The Rasp of War* Sidgewick & Jackson. P. 90

[18] ibid. p. 89

[19] Wilson K. ibid. p. 90

[20] Koss S. (1968) The Destruction of Britain's last Liberal Government. *Journal of Modern History XL* p.257

[21] Pottle M. (1998)*Champion Redoubtable* Phoenix Giant p. 50

[22] Hankey M (1961) *The Supreme Command 1914-1918* George Allen & Unwin p. 315

[23] Pugh. M (1974) Asquith, Bonar Law and the First Coalition *The Historical Journal. XVII, 4, pp 813-836*

[24] Pugh M (1988) *Lloyd George* Longman p. 85

[25] Asquith HH (1919) *The Great Shell Story; Mr Asquith's reply to Lord French* Cassell & Co. ltd.

[26] Cassar G (1994) *Asquith s War Leader* The Hambleton Press. p. 255

[27] Hankey M ibid. p. 312

[28] McGill B (1967) Asquith's Predicament 1914-1918 *The Journal of Modern History* Vol. 39, No. 3 (Sep., 1967), pp. 283-303

[29] Lloyd George D (1938) *Odhams Press Ltd.* Vol 1. PP. 609-615

[30] Beaverbrook. Ibid p. 106

[31] Jenkins R (1964) *Asquith* Collins p. 276

[32] Liverpool Echo - Monday 17 May 1915 Image © Trinity Mirror. Image created courtesy of THE BRITISH LIBRARY BOARD.

[33] Dundee Evening Telegraph - Tuesday 18 May 1915 Image © D.C.Thomson & Co. Ltd. Image created courtesy of THE BRITISH LIBRARY BOARD.

[34] Adams RJQ op cit. p. 185

[35] Fraser P (1982) Lord Beaverbrook's fabrications in *Politicians and the War 1914-1916.* The Historical Journal, 25, 1 pp147-166

[36] Pugh. M (1974) Asquith, Bonar Law and the First Coalition *The Historical Journal. XVII, 4, pp 813-836*

[37] Brock M & E. (1982) *HH Asquith. Letters to Venetia Stanley.* Oxford Press p. 557

[38] Asquith HH (1928) *Memories and Reflections 1852-1927* Little, Brown & Co. Boston. P 117

[39] Wilson T (1966) *The Downfall of the Liberal Party 1914-1935* Collins p. 55

[40] Yorkshire Evening Post - Monday 17 May 1915 Image © Johnston Press plc. Image created courtesy of THE BRITISH LIBRARY BOARD.

[41] Pugh. M (1974) op cit.

[42] Taylor HA (1932) *The Strange Case of Andrew Bonar Law.* Stanley Paul & Co. Ltd. P.212

[43] Sandhurst Lord (1928) *From Day to Day* Edward Arnold & Co. P. 215

[44] Churchill W (1929 *The World Crisis* Odhams Press Ltd. Vol II p. 798

Chapter 8

[1] Gilbert B (1992) *David Lloyd George.* Batsford Ltd. P. 195

[2] Pugh M (1974) <u>Asquith, Bonar Law and the First Coalition</u> *The Historical Journal. XVII, 4, pp 813-836*

[3] Bonar Law to Lloyd George17 May 1915. Lloyd George Papers. Parliamentary Archives. C/5/8/5

[4] Pugh M op cit.

[5] Brock M & E. (2014) *Margot Asquith's Great War Diary 1914-1916* Oxford University Press. Kindle ed. P. CXIVIII

[6] Asquith to Stamfordham 17 May 1915 Asquith Papers. Bodleian Library. Asq.27 fol.162.

[7] Wilson K. (ed) (1988) *The Rasp of War* Sidgewick & Jackson p.

[8] Koss. S (1976) *Asquith* Allen Lane p . 185

[9] Chamberlain to Bonar Law 17 May 1915. Bonar Law Papers Parliamentary Archives BL 37/2/37

[10] HC Deb 19 May 1915 vol 71 cc2392-3

[11] Sandhurst Lord (1928) *From Day to Day* Edward Arnold & Co. P. 210

[12] Riddell Lord (1933) *Lord Riddell's War Diary* Ivor Nicolson & Watson p 87

[13] Ibid p. 90

[14] Brock M & E op cit. loc cit.

[15] op cit. loc cit.

[16] Webb M (ed) (2014) *From Downing Street to the Trenches* Bodleian Library . p. 108

[17] MacCallum Scott, diary, 19 May 1915 University of Glasgow MS Gen 1465/6

[18] Churchill W (1939) *Great Contemporaries* Butler & Tanner. P. 148

[19] Aberdeen Journal - Tuesday 15 June 1915 Image © D.C.Thomson & Co. Ltd. Image created courtesy of THE BRITISH LIBRARY BOARD.

[20] Adelman P (1981) *The Decline of the Liberal Party 1910- 1931* Longman p. 15

[21] Col. Tom Bridges to Bonar Law 18 May 1915 Bonar Law Papers. Parliamentary Archives. BL 37/2/39

[22] HL Deb 13 May 1915 vol 18 cc997-1006

[23] Long to Bonar Law 19 May 1915. Long Papers. British Library Add. Mss. 62404

[24] Bonar Law to Asquith 19 May 1915. Bonar Law Papers. Parliamentary Archives BL 37/5/26

[25] Long to Bonar Law 20 May 1915. Long Papers British Library Add Mss. 62404

[26] Bonar Law to Asquith 21 May 1915 Bonar Law Papers. Parliamentary Archives. BL53/6/3

[27] John Burn's Diary 22 May 1915 Burns Papers, British Library. Add. Mss. 46337

[28] Long to Shadow Cabinet colleagues 22 May 1915. Long Papers. British Library Add. Mss 62419

[29] Wilson T (ed) (1970) *The political diaries of CP Scott 1911-1928* Commins p. 124

[30] Brock M & E (2014) *Margot Asquith's Great War Diary 1914-1916.* Oxford University Press. Kindle Ed. P. CXIVIII

[31]Koss op cit. p. 190

[32] Wilson K. (ed) (1988) *The Rasp of War* Sidgewick & Jackson p. *94*

[33] Long to Asquith 22 May 1915. Long Papers. British Library Add. Mss. 62404

[34] Long W *(1923) Memories* Hutchinson & Co. p. 220-221

[35] Pugh M (1974) Asquith, Bonar Law and the First Coalition *The Historical Journal. XVII, 4, pp 813-836*

[36] Asquith to George V 25 May 1915 Asquith Papers. Bodleian Library Asq. 8

[37] Pottle M. (ed) (1998) *Champion Redoubtable* Phoenix Giant P 57

[38] Hazlehurst C. (1971) *Politicians at War.* Jonathan Cape p. 270

[39] Langan M & Schwarz B (1985) *Crises in the British State.* Hutchinson

[40] John Burns's diary 23 May 1915. Burns Papers. British Library Add. Mss. 46337

[41] Loc cit. 29 May 1915

[42] Loc cit. 30 May 1915

[43] Beaverbrook Lord (1960) *Politicians and the War 1914-1916* Oldbourne Book Co. Ltd. Pp. 134-135

[44] Taylor HA (1932) *The strange case of Andrew Bonar Law.* Stanley Paul & Co. Ltd. P. 215)

[45] Fraser P (1982) Lord Beaverbrook's fabrications in *Politicians and the War 1914-1916.* The Historical Journal, 25, 1 pp.147-166

[46] Long to Bonar Law 30 May 1915 Bonar Law Papers. Parliamentary Archives   BL 50.3.69

Chapter 9

[1] Western Daily Press - Saturday 22 August 1914 Image © Local World Limited. Image created courtesy of THE BRITISH LIBRARY BOARD.

[2] Dundee Courier - Tuesday 06 October 1914 Image © D.C.Thomson & Co. Ltd. Image created courtesy of THE BRITISH LIBRARY BOARD.

[3] Sheffield Evening Telegraph - Wednesday 14 October 1914 Image © Johnston Press plc. Image created courtesy of THE BRITISH LIBRARY BOARD.

[4] Western Daily Press - Wednesday 07 October 1914

Image © Local World Limited. Image created courtesy of THE BRITISH LIBRARY BOARD.

[5] Dundee Courier - Friday 06 November 1914 Image © D.C.Thomson & Co. Ltd. Image created courtesy of THE BRITISH LIBRARY BOARD.

[6] Sheffield Evening Telegraph - Thursday 08 October 1914 Image © Johnston Press plc. Image created courtesy of THE BRITISH LIBRARY BOARD.

[7] Dundee Evening Telegraph - Tuesday 01 December 1914 Image © D.C.Thomson & Co. Ltd. Image created courtesy of THE BRITISH LIBRARY BOARD.

[8] Birmingham Daily Mail - Wednesday 20 January 1915 Image © Trinity Mirror. Image created courtesy of THE BRITISH LIBRARY BOARD.

[9] Aberdeen Journal - Thursday 19 November 1914 Image © D.C.Thomson & Co. Ltd. Image created courtesy of THE BRITISH LIBRARY BOARD.

[10] Derby Daily Telegraph - Saturday 16 January 1915 Image © Local World Limited. Image created courtesy of THE BRITISH LIBRARY BOARD.

[11] Aberdeen Journal - Tuesday 19 January 1915 Image © D.C.Thomson & Co. Ltd. Image created courtesy of THE BRITISH LIBRARY BOARD.

[12] Manchester Evening News - Tuesday 22 December 1914 Image © Trinity Mirror. Image created courtesy of THE BRITISH LIBRARY BOARD.

[13] Manchester Evening News - Wednesday 30 December 1914 Image © Trinity Mirror. Image created courtesy of THE BRITISH LIBRARY BOARD.

[14] Newcastle Journal - Tuesday 05 January 1915 Image © Trinity Mirror. Image created courtesy of THE BRITISH LIBRARY BOARD.

[15] Hull Daily Mail - Monday 11 January 1915 Image © Local World Limited. Image created courtesy of THE BRITISH LIBRARY BOARD.

[16] Glasgow Herald Tuesday 15 June 1915. Bonar Law Papers. Parliamentary Archives BL64/D/4

[17] loc cit.

[18] Daily Record - Wednesday 16 June 1915 Image © Trinity Mirror. Image created courtesy of THE BRITISH LIBRARY BOARD.

[19] Glasgow Herald. Loc cit.

[20] Blake R (1955) *The Unknown Prime Minister* Eyre & Spottiswoode p. 260

[21] Brock M & E (2014) *Margot Asquith's Great War Diary 1914-1916*. Oxford University Press. Kindle Ed. P. CXIVIII

[22] HC Deb 24 June 1915 vol 72 cc1332-3

[23] Blake R op cit. P. 260

[24] Brock M & E (1982) *HH Asquith. Letters to Venetia Stanley.* Oxford Press p. 470

Printed in Great Britain
by Amazon

83233107R10108